# A SNOBOL4 Primer

RALPH E. GRISWOLD

MADGE T. GRISWOLD

*The University of Arizona*

PRENTICE-HALL, INC.

Englewood Cliffs, New Jersey

*Library of Congress Cataloging in Publication Data*

Griswold, Ralph E.
A SNOBOL4 primer.

Includes bibliographical references.
1. SNOBOL (Computer program language)
I. Griswold, Madge T., joint author.
II. Title.
QA76.73.S6G748 001.6'424 73-3307
ISBN 0-13-815381-7



10 9 8 7 6 5 4 3 2 1

Printed in the United States of America

PRENTICE-HALL INTERNATIONAL, INC., *London*
PRENTICE-HALL OF AUSTRALIA, PTY. LTD., *Sydney*
PRENTICE-HALL OF CANADA, LTD., *Toronto*
PRENTICE-HALL OF INDIA PRIVATE LIMITED, *New Delhi*
PRENTICE-HALL OF JAPAN, INC., *Tokyo*

# Contents

# Preface

Most computer programming languages are mainly concerned with numerical computation. SNOBOL4 is unusual in that it is best suited for applications that are not numerical in nature: the manipulation of symbolic expressions, the analysis of text, and the processing of structures. SNOBOL4 is therefore applicable in many areas where the problems are not necessarily of a mathematical nature. Examples are the computer generation and formatting of documents, stylistic analysis, linguistics, and music theory.

Since most programming is done in technical areas, books on computer programming often assume a technical background. This assumption is often implicit; while no specific mathematical background may be required, the terminology and vernacular of mathematics pervade such books. Thus, a person interested in computer programming may be faced with an introductory text that simply assumes that the reader is familiar with terms such as "variable" and "expression". Even the most elementary text can be impenetrable if its vocabulary is alien. Because SNOBOL4 is applicable to many nontechnical problems, there has been a demand for an introduction to SNOBOL4 that does not presume a technical background. That demand motivated this book.

So far as possible, the material is presented here in a way that does not require a familiarity with mathematical or engineering terminology. Of course there are a number of terms that have special meaning in computer programming and in SNOBOL4 in particular. These terms are introduced, and defined in a way that is, we hope, intuitive. Parts of the book touch on technical subjects; that is inescapable. An attempt has been made, however, to keep such material self-contained so that the reader may pick up the information he needs from the book, even if the subject is unfamiliar.

This book is a primer. As such it introduces SNOBOL4 at a relatively simple level. SNOBOL4, taken as a whole, is a complex and sophisticated language. Readers who want to go on to more advanced aspects of SNOBOL4 should read Reference 1, which is a complete description of SNOBOL4 and is also a reference manual.

*Preface*

The material in this book has been developed over a period of time and is a result of teaching SNOBOL4 to individuals with widely varying backgrounds. The authors gratefully acknowledge the encouragement and suggestions of the many persons who have been interested in an elementary book on SNOBOL4. Special appreciation goes to Louis Milic for his insight and for a number of stimulating discussions on the problems of presenting this type of material to students in nontechnical areas. Most of all, our appreciation goes to the many students who have served as guinea pigs for various approaches to teaching programming in SNOBOL4.

We would like to thank Barbara Hyde for her assistance in preparing preliminary drafts. Special thanks go to LeeAnn Underwood for her excellent work in typing the final drafts of the manuscript.

Ralph E. Griswold

Madge T. Griswold

*Tucson, Arizona*

CHAPTER 1

# Introduction

This book is an introduction to computer programming using SNOBOL4. This chapter provides a background by explaining some very basic concepts about computers and computer programming. Readers who are familiar with the use of computers, and who already have some experience in programming, may skip this chapter.

## 1.1 COMPUTERS AND PROGRAMMING

Most people do not have the opportunity to work directly with computers. As a result, there are a number of common misunderstandings about computers. One fairly common misconception is that they are "giant brains"; computers are often viewed as having fantastic intellectual capabilities. In reality, the operations performed by a computer are extremely simple. It is only because these operations are performed very quickly and because computers have a large amount of space for storing information that computers can do anything useful at all. Programming is the process of assembling the simple operations that computers can perform into long, complicated sequences that give the overall effect of sophistication. Essentially, it is the computer programs that are complicated, not the computers themselves.

There is a very wide range of machines that can be called computers. Some are very large, very fast, and control a large amount of other equipment. Others are small, self-contained, and comparatively slow in operation. The structure of most computers can be characterized in the same general terms, although inevitably a general description does not fit any particular computer precisely.

At the heart of a computer is the *central processing unit*, usually referred to as the CPU. The CPU performs the actual computations by executing simple operations called *instructions.* Different kinds of computers have different operation repertoires, called *instruction sets.* Although instruction sets differ in detail, size, variety, and complexity, all basic computer instructions are quite simple. Almost all computers have instructions that add, subtract, multiply, and divide numbers; test and compare results; and select alternate instructions as a result. Whatever differences there are in instruction sets for different kinds of computers, the types of operations are similar and the resulting computation is essentially the same. The user of a computer can think of the CPU as a "black box" that performs simple computations in some manner. He does not have to be concerned with the details of how this is accomplished.

A CPU in itself is virtually useless. A computer must have a place to store the data to be processed and a place to put results. For this purpose computers have memories, which are simply storage places for data. The CPU can fetch information from memory and store information back into memory. There are usually a variety of CPU instructions for moving data to and from memory. Figure 1.1 illustrates this situation schematically. The word "data", incidentally, is commonly used in computer-related areas for both singular and plural forms.

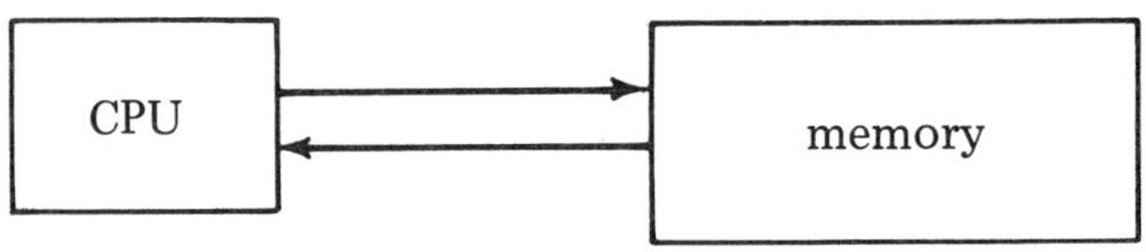


**Figure 1.1** The Central Part of a Computer

In addition to memory, computers need access to other information. Additional storage is provided for information that need not be readily available or is too massive to fit into memory all at once. This *secondary storage* usually consists of magnetic tapes, magnetic disks, and magnetic drums. Enormous amounts of information can be stored on such devices, and in some cases they can be removed from the computer for storage or transmission elsewhere.

Even with secondary storage, a computer would be essentially isolated from the rest of the world if there were no means of communicating with individuals who use and run it. There are various forms of communication. One is the computer console which usually has buttons, switches, and a typewriter-like keyboard. Through this console, the computer may be controlled by operators.

Individual users also need to communicate with the computer. This communication may be performed in a variety of ways. The most common method requires information to be punched on cards, which are then read into the computer through a card reader. Similarly, the results produced by a computer are usually printed and returned to the user on paper, called *printout.* This means of using a computer isolates the user from the computer to the extent that he may never see it. He only places decks of cards on a counter and receives printed paper in return. There are also communication devices that permit the user to enter data directly into the computer and, in return, to receive the computer response directly. The most common communication device, or *terminal*, is the Teletype ®. There are many kinds of terminals, including those that provide video displays on screens similar to television consoles. With a terminal, access to a computer can be obtained through telephone lines. Hence the user may be physically remote from the computer he uses. The general relationship among the components described above is shown schematically in Figure 1.2. This figure is intended to illustrate typical relationships; specific configurations vary considerably.

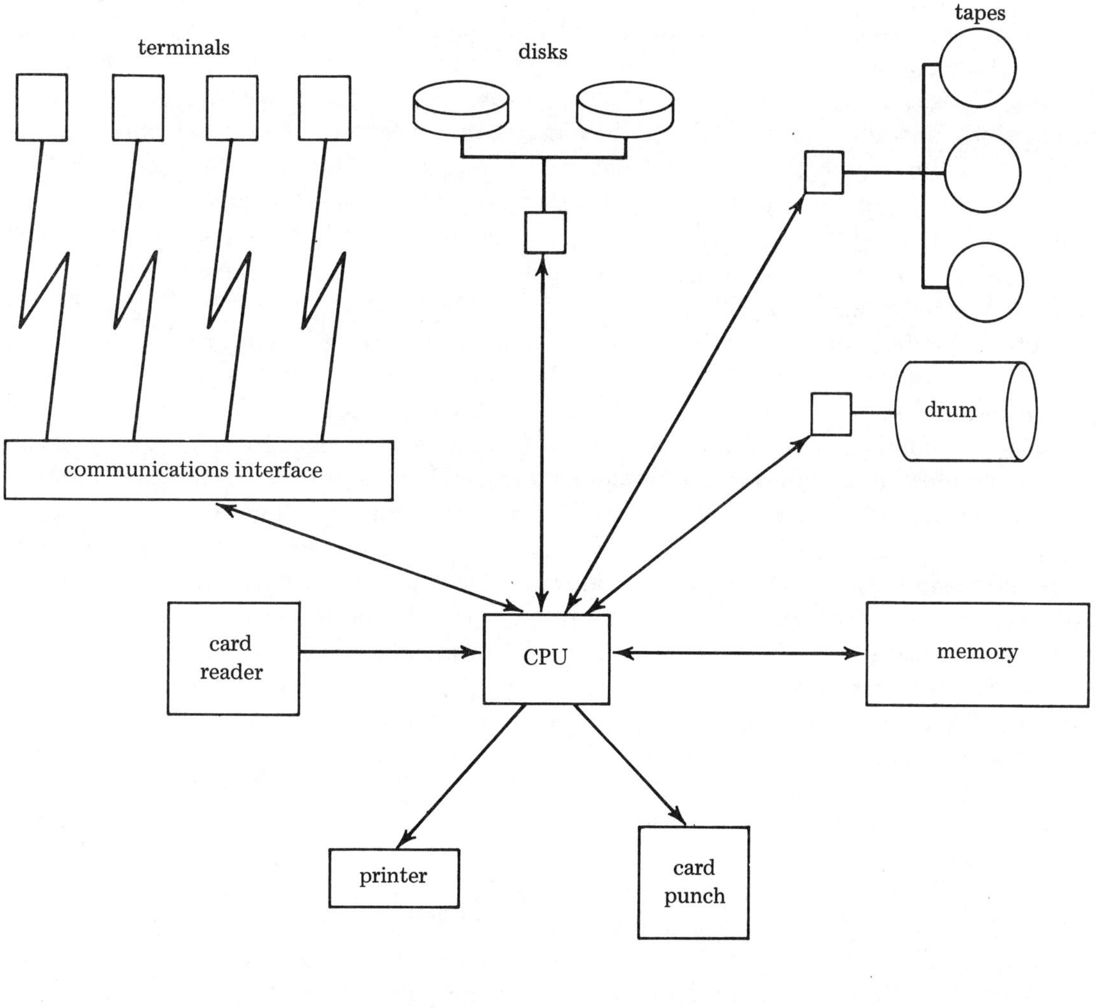


**Figure 1.2** A Typical Computer Configuration

As computers have grown in sophistication, the number of different components and interconnections between them have become more complex. It is quite common for a large computer to have several CPUs operating simultaneously, either independently or cooperatively. On an even larger scale, computer networks have been developed in which many computers, physically far apart, are connected through communication lines. In spite of this complexity, the basic operation of a computer remains the same: a user can provide information and direction, the computer performs the operations that it is instructed to perform, and the results are returned to the user.

## 1.2 PROGRAMS AND PROGRAMMING LANGUAGES

CPU instructions are, individually, quite simple. No single instruction does very much. Many instructions, executed in a given order, can perform very elaborate tasks. An assemblage of instructions is called a program. A program specifies the individual instructions and the order in which they are to be executed. The CPU executes the program and, in conjunction with its related components, produces the results.

To solve a problem on a computer, the user must write a program which, when executed, will produce the desired answer. This requires a precise description of the individual instructions to be carried out in solving the problem. Such a description is called an algorithm. Computers do not know how to solve problems; they can only execute a limited number of different, and very simple, instructions. Therefore an algorithm must be so complete and detailed that it can be carried out without any understanding of what the problem is or what result is desired. To use a computer to solve a problem, the programmer must formulate the solution as an algorithm; a precise, unambiguous, and completely detailed method.

To illustrate the meaning of the word algorithm, consider the following example. Suppose examination papers have been scored on a numerical scale and are to be sorted into piles according to the letter-grade equivalent of the score. This process is so simple that a brief verbal description would be sufficient to tell a person how to sort the papers. Such a description might be: "if the score is 90 or greater, it's an A, between 80 and 90, a B, between 70 and 80, a C, between 60 and 70 a D, less than that is an F." An algorithm, on the other hand, must be more specific and must provide details that are unnecessary when instructing a person. An algorithm might have the form:

1. Select the next examination paper. If there is none, stop. Otherwise proceed to step 2.
2. If the score on the selected paper is 90 or greater, place the paper in the A pile and go to step 1. Otherwise proceed to step 3.
3. If the score on the selected paper is 80 or greater, place the paper in the B pile and go to step 1. Otherwise proceed to step 4.

4. If the score on the selected paper is 70 or greater, place the paper in the C pile and go to step 1. Otherwise proceed to step 5.

5. If the score on the selected paper is 60 or greater, place the paper in the D pile and go to step 1. Otherwise proceed to step 6.

6. Place the paper in the F pile and go to step 1.

This algorithm is tediously protracted, but it illustrates what is involved in a precise description of a process. Notice, for example, that step 1 contains an explicit instruction about what to do when all the papers have been processed. Such an instruction would ordinarily be unnecessary if a person were sorting papers, but a computer must be given precise instructions for every situation. The algorithm given above does not, in fact, allow for every possible situation. Suppose a paper has no score, or that the score is not a number, but perhaps a letter grade already. Such cases often have to be considered in practice. The fact that computers carry out instructions quite literally can be an annoyance. In the example above, a paper that has a score of A, rather than a numerical score, would likely wind up in the F pile. On the other hand, a score of A might cause an error in a program that is expecting numbers. Such results are not computer malfunctions, but the result of an error, an omission in the algorithm.

The way an algorithm is stated depends on the operations that can be performed. The algorithm above contains operations like "select" and "place" and assumes the ability to read scores and compare them in a numerical scale. An algorithm is not precise and unambiguous unless the terms in it correspond to operations that can be executed on a computer. This algorithm is written in English, not the instructions of a computer. The algorithm written directly for a computer would be much more detailed and virtually incomprehensible to a person who is not intimately familiar with the computer's instructions.

To specify a computer solution in this way, using individual, very simple, instructions, would be tedious and difficult. A large number of computer instructions have to be written for even a simple program. Many millions of instructions may have to be executed to solve a problem on a computer. The instructions themselves are quite detailed and are closely related to the specific internal structure of the computer. Moreover, computer instructions are often far removed, in their form, from the problem to be solved. Hence, it is usually inappropriate to use them directly. For these reasons, most computer programs are not written using the instructions of the computer. Instead, systems have been developed to permit the users of computers to write operations more suitable for expressing their algorithms. These operations are automatically translated into the instruction set of the computer and are executed by the computer. Consequently, most users of computers do not need to know the actual computer instructions. The algorithm can be stated using operations which are appropriate to the problem. These operations constitute a language which is called a *programming language*.

Programming languages characteristically include operations that are quite sophisticated, and many times more powerful and comprehensive than the individual machine instructions. Thus, an algorithm usually can be stated in a programming language much more easily than it could be stated in the instruction set of the computer. A further advantage of programming languages results from the fact that different computers have different instruction sets. If a program is written using the instruction set of one computer, that program is virtually useless on another computer. Programming languages, however, usually do not depend directly on a particular computer. Translators have been written so that programming languages can be used on different types of computers. A program written in a programming language can be largely independent of the type of computer on which it is developed. Such a program often can be run with only a few modifications on an entirely different type of computer.

On first sight, one might ask why a special type of language is necessary for writing programs; why not just use English or some other natural language? This possibility has been given considerable attention, but, in spite of its apparent advantages, it has not turned out to be practical in most circumstances. Unfortunately, natural languages are ambiguous and imprecise. The same word may have different meanings in different contexts. A computer has no way of determining the precise meaning of a word necessary to perform the desired operation. Human beings, despite years of experience and the ability to perform complex processes, are often unable to determine the precise meaning of even simple sentences. Furthermore, natural languages are highly redundant. This is useful for human communication, but becomes burdensome in performing even simple processes on a computer. Refer to the algorithm given above if this is not clear. Finally, many computations that are best performed on a computer involve technical subjects that natural languages are poorly equipped to describe. For these reasons, programming languages have been developed to allow concise and unambiguous formulation of algorithms for solving a variety of technical and nontechnical problems.

There are many programming languages—hundreds, in fact. Only a few dozen are in common use, however. Most programming is done in about ten languages which are the most popular. These languages differ considerably in their design and purpose. Some are intended primarily for numerical computation. FORTRAN (Formula Translator) is the most widely used language in this area. COBOL (Common Business Oriented Language) is designed for business applications. Algol (Algorithmic Language) is designed for scientific applications. More recently, PL/I (Programming Language One) has entered the field as a competitor for both scientific and business applications. APL (A Programming Language) is particularly oriented toward direct, conversational interaction with the computer through a communications terminal. The reader who is interested in more information about programming languages should see Reference 2.

The languages listed above are essentially general-purpose languages in the sense that they are applicable to a wide variety of problems, even though they vary in the emphasis that they place on certain types of operations and applications. Other languages are designed for special purposes, such as the simulation of processes or events. Languages differ in the power and sophistication of the operations they provide. Some are high-level languages, providing operations that are powerful and complex. Others are low-level, providing operations closer to the nature of the instruction set of the computer.

This book is an introduction to SNOBOL4 (String Oriented Symbolic Language). SNOBOL4 is a high-level, general-purpose language, but it has a strong emphasis on operations that involve symbols and structures, as opposed to numbers. Thus SNOBOL4 is especially applicable to problems that involve analyzing text, manipulating mathematical formulas, creating documents, and so forth.

The operations of the SNOBOL4 language are a long way indeed from the instruction set of the computer. It is not necessary to understand anything about computer instructions themselves to use SNOBOL4. SNOBOL4 translators have been written for most of the major large-scale computers in current use. Consequently SNOBOL4 programs can be run on a variety of computers.

## 1.3 SCOPE OF THE BOOK

This book is a primer, an introduction to SNOBOL4. No previous programming experience is required (such experience, of course, will help). In any programming language, as with the computer itself, a problem solution must be formulated as an algorithm and this algorithm must then be expressed in the operations of the programming language. The purpose of this book is to describe the operations of SNOBOL4. Once these operations have been learned, the reader may apply them to his own problems. This book is more concerned with the operations of SNOBOL4 and how to use them than it is with the development of algorithms. There are many examples in the book, however, which suggest approaches to formulating algorithms.

The book does not describe the entire SNOBOL4 language, but only the basic parts that are needed for writing most programs. In addition to the operations described here, there are a number of more advanced operations that some programmers may find interesting. The entire SNOBOL4 language is described in detail in Reference 1. Reference 1 is also a complete reference manual, and serious SNOBOL4 programmers may find it useful for this reason. For more information on methods of problem solution and problems to which SNOBOL4 is particularly applicable, Reference 3 may be of interest. Those curious about how SNOBOL4 translators are written should see Reference 4.

The remainder of this book is devoted to SNOBOL4. Chapter 2 describes the basic features of SNOBOL4, introducing various operations and the format of the language. Chapters 3 through 7 provide more detail and describe other features. Chapter 8 discusses programming techniques and Chapter 9 describes methods of correcting errors in programs. Appendices include reference material and solutions to the exercises that appear at the ends of chapters.

This book is designed to be tutorial, and as such it tries to make the material understandable. As a consequence, some precision, detail, and technical accuracy have been sacrificed. The reader should refer to Reference 1 if he is in doubt about a specific case.

A final word concerns the use of the book. A computer is a device for solving problems and producing results. A programming language is a way of formulating a solution for computer processing, not an abstract mathematical entity. If at all possible, write programs and actually run them on a computer. There is no better way to gain an intuitive feeling and a complete understanding for a programming language or for the process of programming itself.

CHAPTER 2

# The Basics of SNOBOL4

To learn how to use a programming language, it is necessary to learn the way that the programming language refers to data to be processed and the kind of operations that can be performed. This chapter covers the basic aspects of SNOBOL4 and introduces the most important concepts in an elementary way. By the end of this chapter, simple but complete programs can be written. Subsequent chapters go into more detail and introduce more advanced operations.

## 2.1 INTEGERS AND STRINGS

### Integers

Integers are used for counting and computing numerical results, and may be positive, negative, or zero. Integers in SNOBOL4 are written in much the same way as they are in conventional long-hand notation, except that commas are not used for separating groups of three digits as they usually are in writing or printing. Examples are 1, 36, 37520, -42, 0, and -2000.

### Strings

Any single symbol is called a *character*. The letters A, B, and so forth are examples. So are the symbols $, /, and *. A *string* is a sequence of characters, strung together, one after another. For example, AB is a string of two characters: A followed by B. The individual characters are important, as well as the order in which they occur. For example, BA is a different string than AB.

A string may be very long, or it may consist of only one character. For example, A is a one-character string. A string may even consist of no characters, although there is no way to illustrate such a string. The string consisting of no characters is called the *null string.* This rather curious string is surprisingly useful, and it appears a number of times later in this book. The number of characters in a string is called the length of the string. The length of ABC is three; the length of the null string is zero.

Since strings consist of characters, they are useful for representing words, sentences, mathematical expressions, and, in general, any kind of written or printed material. For this reason, programs that process such material must manipulate strings. Most programming languages place more emphasis on numbers than on strings, and some languages even have no direct way of handling strings. SNOBOL4, on the other hand, has powerful facilities for processing strings and it is sometimes referred to as a string-manipulation language. Actually SNOBOL4 can handle many types of data, not just strings and numbers. However, it is very effective in dealing with strings. Hence, SNOBOL4 is a good language to use for problems that involve data that can naturally be represented as strings.

In SNOBOL4 programs, data strings are enclosed in quotation marks. For example, the string AB is written 'AB'. The quotation marks serve as delimiters, marking the beginning and end of the string. A quoted string is called a *literal* since the string is written out literally. The quotation marks themselves are not part of the string. The importance of the quotation marks is illustrated by the literal ' AB ' which begins and ends with a blank. Without the quotation marks, the blanks would be "invisible" and it would be difficult, if not impossible, to determine where the string begins and ends. Actually there are other, equally important, reasons for using quotation marks. Data strings are written in programs that contain other symbols standing for program operations and so forth. Thus, the delimiting quotation marks set data strings off from the rest of the program.

Any kind of character may occur in a data string. The letters and numerals are used most frequently, but other symbols may be used also. The blank, which has no visible representation, is an example; mathematical operators and punctuation marks are others. In data strings, all characters are equally important, or unimportant, depending on your viewpoint. The blank is just as much a character as the letter A, although the two may stand for different things when used in data.

Double quotation marks may also be used to delimit data strings. Both "OWL-EYED" and 'OWL-EYED' specify the same data string. The closing quotation mark must be the same as the opening one. As mentioned, the delimiting quotation marks are not part of the data string. If one kind of quotation mark is needed in a data string, the other kind of quotation mark can be used to delimit the literal. An example is:

```
'HE APPEARS TO BE "OWL-EYED".'
```

In this example, the double quotation marks are part of the data string, but the delimiting single quotation marks are not. Similarly, a single quotation mark is often used to represent an apostrophe. An example is:

```
"THAT'S OUR MAN"
```

The characters that may be used in data strings depend on the kind of computer you are using. Each machine has its own *character set* which consists of all the characters available on that computer. Almost all computers provide upper-case letters, numerals, the blank, the common arithmetic symbols, parentheses, and a few punctuation marks. In this book the following characters are used in SNOBOL4 programs:

```
ABCDEFGHIJKLMNOPQRSTUVWXYZ0123456789+-/*(),.$='"&<>|!;
```

and the blank.

## 2.2 ASSIGNMENT

During execution of a typical program, many values may be computed. Most of the values that are computed are intermediate results which lead up to final results of the program. Often many values must be kept available for use in later computations. The program, however, can generate only one value at a time. A value may be assigned to a *name*, and then subsequently may be referred to by using the identifying name. Thus a name provides a way of keeping track of a value.

A value is associated with a name by performing an *assignment*. An assignment has the form:

*name* = *value*

At least one blank is required on each side of the equal sign to separate it from the name and the value. More blanks may be used if desired. Blanks are used in a number of situations to separate components. In this book, the number of blanks used to separate components is chosen to produce a uniform format. An example of an assignment is

```
FIRST = 25
```

which *assigns* the *value* 25 to the *name* FIRST. Subsequently, FIRST may be used to reference this value. For example

```
SECOND = FIRST
```

assigns the value 25 to the name SECOND also.

String values also may be assigned to names. An example is

```
WORD = 'REVERE'
```

which assigns the string REVERE to the name WORD.

Names begin with a letter and may be followed by any number of other letters, numerals, or periods. Examples are, SERENDIPITY, X, X.3, Q3, and K2Z7. Appropriately chosen names are a great help in developing a program and in making it intelligible to others. While names in SNOBOL4 have no meaning in themselves, the names used in examples in this book are chosen to suggest the types of values they have. Names like WORD and TEXT are used when dealing with language examples, for instance. Following the convention of mathematics, names such as I, J, K, M, and N are often used for integers, and so forth.

The null string may be assigned to a name by omitting the value altogether. An example is

```
          TEXT    =
```

which assigns the null string to TEXT. When program execution is started, names have null strings as their initial values. Only later are they assigned other values as execution proceeds. Therefore, assigning the null string to a name restores that name to its original condition. This assignment is often used when a new series of computations is started after one series is complete.

The value assigned to a name may be changed by subsequent assignments. For example

```
          TEXT    =    WORD
```

changes the value of TEXT to REVERE.

The use of the equal sign for assignment deserves an explanation. In mathematical contexts, the equal sign is used to indicate that two expressions have the same value. In SNOBOL4, the equal sign causes an action that associates a name with a value. The reason for using the equal sign to denote this association is simple: on most computers there is no better character. An arrow pointing to the left would be more descriptive and would avoid the confusion with the mathematical use of the equal sign. Unfortunately most character sets do not have a left arrow, or if they do, it is not available on devices used to prepare programs.

### Variables

The name to which a value is assigned is sometimes called a *variable*. This term is derived from mathematics in which an equation contains variables (typically X, Y, and Z) whose values are sought in solution of the equation. In a programming language, it may be helpful to think of a variable as something whose value may vary during program execution.

Some variables are more complicated than the names used above; keywords are an example. A keyword is identified by an ampersand (&) followed by a name that has a special meaning. For example, &ALPHABET is a keyword whose value is a string consisting of the computer's character set. Another keyword is &DUMP. If a positive integer is assigned to &DUMP by an assignment such as

```
&DUMP    =    1
```

a listing of all names and their values is printed at the end of the program run. Keywords are variables and have values just like names chosen by the programmer. The names of keywords, however, are fixed, and each has a special, predetermined meaning. There are a variety of keywords described in appropriate sections throughout this book. There are also other kinds of variables which are described later.

## 2.3 EXPRESSIONS

Operators are used for performing arithmetic and other operations. One of the most common operations is addition, indicated by the operator +. Two integers to be added are written on either side of the operator. Thus 7 + 3 indicates the addition of the integers 7 and 3. Notation such as this indicates that an *operation* is to be performed and is called an *expression.* The result of performing the operation is called the *value* of the expression. Not surprisingly, the value of the expression above is the integer 10.

Expressions can be used to compute values assigned to names. If the value of FIRST is 25, then

```
SECOND    =    FIRST + 7
```

assigns the value 32 to SECOND.

In fact, the name to which the value is assigned may be used in the expression which computes the value. An example is:

```
SECOND    =    SECOND + 1
```

First the expression on the right side of the equal sign is evaluated. Since the value of SECOND is presently 32, the result is 33. Now the assignment is made, changing the value of SECOND to 33. In effect the assignment adds 1 to the value of SECOND.

Most arithmetic operations are written in SNOBOL4 in a way similar to that used in ordinary notation. The operator symbols are +, -, *, and / for addition, subtraction, multiplication, and division respectively. These operators are called *binary operators* because they have two operands. Thus 7 + 3 is a binary operation on the operands 7 and 3. In SNOBOL4, binary operators must be surrounded by blanks as shown. That is, there must be at least one blank between the 7 and the + and at least one blank between the + and the 3. More than one blank is permitted, but at least one is required. An expression may contain more than one operator. An example is 7 * 3 * 2 which has the value 42.

Parentheses may be used to group the components of an expression. Such grouping is particularly helpful in clarifying the structure of complicated expressions and in assuring that the correct operations are performed. An example of an expression containing parenthesized groupings is:

```
(7 * 3) - (5 + (6 / 2))
```

As indicated by this example, parenthesized expressions may be nested. Thus, (6 / 2) is nested within a larger grouping.

Operations may be performed on strings as well as integers. A string is a sequence of characters. One string appended to another is also a sequence of characters and, hence, is also a string. The operation of appending one string to another is called *concatenation.* If the string DEF is concatenated on the end of the string ABC the result is the string ABCDEF. Most operations are indicated by a symbol such as +. However, concatenation is performed so frequently in SNOBOL4 that no symbol is used to indicate it. Strings to be concatenated are simply written down, one after another, with one or more blanks separating them. Thus

```
HEADING    =    'THE RESULT IS ' WORD
```

concatenates a literal string and the value of WORD. If the value of WORD is the string COMPLETE, the value assigned to HEADING is:

```
THE RESULT IS COMPLETE
```

Observe that the blanks in this string are as important as the other characters. If the literal string had not ended with a blank, the value of HEADING would have been:

```
THE RESULT ISCOMPLETE
```

As illustrated by this example, blanks may appear in data strings and may also be used to separate strings that are to be concatenated. Do not confuse the two uses of blanks.

Another example of concatenation is

```
GRADES    =    GRADES 'W'
```

which has the effect of appending a W to the value of GRADES. This is accomplished by concatenating a W onto the previous value of GRADES and then assigning the newly formed string as the new value of GRADES. If the previous value of GRADES was ABCDF, the new value is ABCDFW. Note that the new value of GRADES is longer than its former value. In SNOBOL4, changes of length are taken care of automatically.

Several strings may be concatenated in the same expression. An example is

```
TEXT    =    WORD1 ' ' WORD2 ' ' WORD3 ' ' WORD4
```

which concatenates seven strings together. The result is the value of the four named strings separated by blanks. Note the difference between the blanks in data strings and the blanks indicating concatenation. With a little practice, it becomes easy to tell what is inside quotation marks and what is outside them.

## 2.4 BUILT-IN FUNCTIONS

There are many kinds of operations that can be performed on numbers and strings. For example, it is often useful to be able to find out how long a string is. SNOBOL4 provides a number of functions for such purposes. A function computes a value which depends on (i.e. is a *function* of) its *arguments.* The length of a string, for example, is a function of that string.

In SNOBOL4, a function has an identifying name followed by parentheses enclosing its arguments. The function that computes the length of a string has the name SIZE. The following statement computes the length of WORD and assigns it to L.

```
L    =    SIZE(WORD)
```

If the value of WORD is the string INDIVIDUAL, the value assigned to L is 10. The left parenthesis must immediately follow the name of the function; otherwise the separating blanks would indicate concatenation.

Some functions have values that depend on more than one argument. The remainder which results from the division of two numbers is an illustration. If a function has more than one argument, the arguments are separated by commas. REMDR is the name of the function that computes remainders. Therefore

```
R    =    REMDR(37,11)
```

assigns to R the remainder of the division of 37 by 11, namely 4.

When a function is encountered during program execution, it is evaluated. This evaluation is referred to as a *function call.* The result of a function call is a value which can be used in other computations just like any other value. This value is called the *value returned* by the function call. For example, the statement

```
C    =    12 + REMDR(50,12)
```

calls the function REMDR. The value returned is 2, which is then added to 12. As a result, 14 is assigned to C. A function call is itself an expression. In the example above, the function call is an operand of the addition operation.

Consider the following assignments.

```
L    =   SIZE(TEXT)

SWITCH    =    REMDR(L,2)
```

If the length of TEXT is even, 0 is assigned to SWITCH, but if the length of TEXT is odd, 1 is assigned to SWITCH. The value of one function call can be used as the argument of another. Thus the two assignments above can be combined into a single statement:

```
SWITCH    =    REMDR(SIZE(TEXT),2)
```

Here the first argument of REMDR is a function call, SIZE(TEXT). Thus one function call is "nested" within another. Any argument of any function may be an expression, no matter how complicated that expression is.

SNOBOL4 has many such functions that do a variety of things. These functions are described in later sections as new subjects are introduced. All functions have the form described here.

Functions that are part of SNOBOL4 are called *built-in functions.* SNOBOL4 also has provisions for defining new functions that are not part of the SNOBOL4 system. These programmer-defined functions are described in Chapter 5.

## 2.5 STATEMENTS AND THE SEQUENCE OF EXECUTION

A SNOBOL4 program consists of a sequence of statements:

statement 1

statement 2

statement 3

.

.

.

These statements may do a variety of things: assign values to names, read in data, perform computations, compare values, print out results, and so on. The preceding sections illustrate statements that perform computations and assign values. Other types of statements are illustrated in later sections. Statements are executed in sequence, one after another, in the order in which they are written.

Sometimes it is useful to stop the sequential execution of statements at one place in a program and begin executing statements elsewhere. Altering the sequential execution of statements is called *transfer of control* and is accomplished by performing a *goto* to a specified statement. The term goto refers to the program operation that transfers control. (Admittedly goto is an inelegant term, but is part of the established jargon.)

A goto is written at the end of a statement and is separated from the rest of the statement by a colon. Following the colon are parentheses that enclose a *label* identifying the statement to which control is to be transferred. Any statement may have an identifying label so that control can be transferred to it. A label is placed at the beginning of a statement. If the program is punched on cards, the label must start in column one.

Labels are ordinarily composed of the same characters as names. Examples are Q, LOOP, PRINT3, and START.1. A blank indicates the end of the label and separates it from the rest of the statement. A statement without a label begins with a blank. Characters other than letters, numerals, and periods also may appear in labels. See Appendix A. Labels may be chosen by the programmer to suit his fancy. The characters have no significance to SNOBOL4, but appropriate choices, indicating what the labeled statements are supposed to do, are very helpful in reading the program. The choice of appropriate mnemonics for labels as well as for names is a principle of good programming. Each label must be different.

Consider the following sketch of a program in which the statements are numbered on the right for reference.

```
        BOTTOM  =  0                                        1
        TOP  =  BOTTOM + 100                                2
        RESULT  =  0                                        3
CALC    TOP  =  TOP + 1                                     4
        .                                                   .
        .                                                   .
        .                                                   .
        RESULT  =  RESULT + 1                  :(CALC)      32
        .                                                   .
        .                                                   .
        .                                                   .
```

In this hypothetical program, statements 4 through 31 presumably perform some desired calculation. Statement 32 increments the value of RESULT and has a goto which transfers control back to statement 4, which is labeled CALC. Such a goto is called an *unconditional goto*. After statement 32 is executed, control is always transferred to statement 4. Control can be transferred to any statement in the program, not just to an earlier statement.

A statement with a label may be *flowed into* from above as well as reached by a transfer. In the example above, after statement 3 is executed, control flows into statement 4.

The last statement in a program is identified by the special label END. Execution of a program is terminated by a transfer to END, or by flowing into END.

## 2.6 CONDITIONAL OPERATIONS

If there were only unconditional gotos, programs would not be very interesting. SNOBOL4, however, has a number of operations that test conditions, compare values, and so forth. Such operations are called *conditional operations* and may *succeed* or *fail* depending on conditions that exist in the program. When a conditional operation succeeds, program execution continues in the normal way. When a conditional operation fails, however, the execution of the current statement stops when the operation fails, even if the statement contains other computations to be performed. The statement is said to *fail* in this case.

There is a special class of functions in SNOBOL4 called *predicates*. A predicate has arguments like a regular function, but instead of computing a value, it succeeds or fails depending on the relationship between the values of its arguments. Different predicates test different relationships. Examples are IDENT and DIFFER. IDENT succeeds if its arguments have identical values and fails if they do not. DIFFER is the opposite of IDENT, and succeeds if its arguments do not have identical values. For example

```
        IDENT(FIRST,SECOND)
```

succeeds only if the value of FIRST is identical to the value of SECOND. In the example above, if the value of FIRST is ABC and the value of SECOND is ABCD, IDENT fails. Transfer can be made conditional on successful completion or on failure of a statement. Such gotos are called *conditional gotos* and are identified by an S (for success) or an F (for failure) before the parentheses enclosing the label. When a predicate fails, it stops execution of the statement in which it occurs and a failure goto is selected if one is present. For example

```
        IDENT(FIRST,SECOND)                           :S(YES)
```

transfers to YES if FIRST and SECOND are identical. If FIRST and SECOND are not identical, execution continues with the next statement. Trailing arguments that are omitted in a function call are assumed to be null strings. Therefore

```
        IDENT(FIRST)                                  :S(YES)
```

transfers to YES if the value of FIRST is null.

A statement may have both a success and a failure goto. For example

```
        IDENT(FIRST,SECOND)                           :F(NO)S(YES)
```

transfers to YES if FIRST and SECOND are identical, but transfers to NO otherwise. If a statement has both a success and a failure goto, the two gotos may be written in either order.

In general, functions compute values that depend on their arguments. If a predicate fails, no value is returned, and statement execution terminates. On the other hand, if a predicate succeeds, it returns a null string as value. This convention is useful in programming, since null strings usually vanish from computations without having any effect. The typical example is concatenation of the null string onto another string. The result is the same as if the null string had not been there. For this reason, a predicate can be inserted into an expression to make evaluation of the expression conditional on the success of the predicate. An example is the statement:

```
        APPEND    =    DIFFER(FIRST,SECOND) FIRST SECOND
```

If FIRST and SECOND are different, the value of APPEND becomes the result of concatenating FIRST and SECOND. If FIRST and SECOND are identical, the concatenation is not performed and the value of APPEND is not changed.

There are a number of predicates that compare the sizes of numbers. For example, EQ succeeds if the values of its two arguments are numerically equal. Similarly LT succeeds if its first argument is less than its second. Such predicates are useful in performing a calculation that is to be repeated a number of times. Suppose, for example, that several copies of a string are to be concatenated together. If the number of copies desired in the value of M and the string to be concatenated is the value of S, the following statements compute the desired result.

```
         COPIES   =

         N   =   1

AGAIN    COPIES   =   COPIES S

         N   =   LT(N,M)  N + 1                          :S(AGAIN)

         .

         .

         .
```

First the value of COPIES is made null in case it had a previous value. N is used to count the number of copies and is initially set to 1. The first time the statement labeled AGAIN is executed, the original null value of COPIES is concatenated with the value of S, which results in the value of S. On subsequent executions of AGAIN, copies of S are appended to COPIES. Following execution of AGAIN, the value of N is incremented. Provided N is less than M, the predicate succeeds and returns a null value. In this case the statement is equivalent to:

```
        N    =    N + 1                                  :(AGAIN)
```

When N finally becomes as large as M, the predicate fails and execution continues with the next statement in the program. At that time, COPIES contains the desired result.

The segment of program given above is typical of the way that operations are performed *iteratively* in SNOBOL4. A *loop* of statements is set up with a conditional test to determine when the computation is complete. Of course, care must be taken that the values used in the conditional test are set up properly. Consider what happens in the example above if the value of M is 0.

## 2.7 PATTERN MATCHING

Strings of characters can be used to represent many different kinds of data. To manipulate such strings, it is often necessary to examine them to determine the various properties they have. For example, one might want to determine whether a string contains specific characters, whether it begins or ends with a certain character, and so on. The examination of the structure of a string is called *pattern matching*. SNOBOL4 is best known for its pattern-matching facilities, which are very elaborate and powerful. In fact most of the SNOBOL4 language is composed of pattern-matching operations.

In SNOBOL4, pattern matching is accomplished by writing the string to be examined, called the *subject*, in the position where a name appears in an assignment statement. The *pattern* is written next, using blanks to separate the two. Thus a pattern-matching statement has the form:

*subject pattern*

The simplest type of pattern matching consists of examining one string to see if it contains another string. An example is:

```
TEXT     'A'
```

This pattern-matching statement examines the value of TEXT to see if it contains the letter A. If the letter A occurs anywhere in the value of TEXT, the pattern match succeeds. Otherwise it fails. For example, if the value of TEXT is HALLOWEEN, the pattern match succeeds, but if the value of TEXT is MYSTERY, the pattern match fails. This success or failure may be used to select a conditional branch. A slightly more complicated example is illustrated by the statement:

```
TEXT     'AL'                                   :S(FOUND)
```

In this statement, the pattern match succeeds only if AL is a substring in TEXT, that is if the two characters AL occur consecutively in the value of TEXT. AL is a substring in HALLOWEEN but not in ATOLL. If the pattern match succeeds, control is transferred to FOUND. Otherwise the next statement in line is executed.

Sometimes it is useful to know if a string is matched by one pattern or by another, alternate, pattern. Such a test could be done in two statements, but that is unnecessary because SNOBOL4 allows alternatives to be included in a pattern. The binary operator | indicates alternatives. For example, the statement

```
TEXT    'AL'  |  'LA'
```

succeeds if TEXT contains either the substring AL or the substring LA. Many alternatives can be given in a single pattern. For example

```
TEXT    'A'  |  'E'  |  'I'  |  'O'  |  'U'
```

might be used to determine if TEXT contains a vowel, assuming a vowel is defined to be an A, E, I, O, or U.

It is not necessary for a pattern to be written out in every statement in which it is used. It can be assigned to a variable like any other value. For example, the statement

```
VOWEL   =   'A'  |  'E'  |  'I'  |  'O'  |  'U'
```

assigns a *pattern* VOWEL. Subsequently this pattern may be referred to by the name VOWEL as in the statement

```
TEXT    VOWEL
```

which performs the same operation as that in the previous pattern-matching statement. Assigning patterns to names saves a lot of writing when the same pattern is used in a number of places in the program. Well-chosen names for patterns can also be helpful in making a program understandable, since patterns may become so complicated that it is difficult to tell what they do simply by looking at them.

Patterns may be concatenated in the same way that strings are concatenated. For example, the statement

```
TEXT    VOWEL 'T'
```

succeeds if a vowel is immediately followed by a T in TEXT, i.e. if TEXT contains one of the substrings AT, ET, IT, OT, or UT. Another example is the statement

```
TEXT    VOWEL VOWEL
```

which succeeds only if TEXT contains a substring consisting of two vowels in a row. Here there are 25 possibilities starting with AA and ending with UU. This example illustrates how easily a relatively complicated set of alternatives can be constructed from a simple pattern.

All the patterns discussed above are constructed from strings of characters. There are also patterns that do not depend on specific strings. One of these is the value of a built-in function, LEN. LEN produces a pattern that matches a string of characters whose length is determined by the value of its argument. For example, LEN(1) produces a pattern that matches any string of length 1; LEN(2), any string of length 2; and so on.

Consider the statement:

```
TEXT    'T' LEN(2) 'N'
```

If T matches, the pattern produced by LEN(2) simply matches the next two characters. If the next character is N, the pattern match succeeds. Therefore if the value of TEXT is

```
THEN THE CURTAIN FELL
```

the pattern match succeeds, matching the substring THEN. The pattern produced by LEN(2) matches *any* two characters. Thus the pattern above would also match strings such as THIN, TEEN, TORN, and even T**N. Patterns produced by LEN fail if there are not enough characters to match. For example, a pattern produced by LEN(30) would fail to match the value of TEXT given above.

This is only the barest introduction to pattern matching. There are many other types of patterns that can be used to determine the structure of a string and to locate substructures within it. These matters are the subject of Chapter 4.

## 2.8 VALUE ASSIGNMENT IN PATTERN MATCHING

Pattern matching provides a way of examining strings to determine their structures. However, many patterns can match more than one string. Even the simple pattern VOWEL described in Section 2.7 can match five different strings. Pattern matching itself provides no way of determining *which* string is matched. In order to find out which string is matched, a name may be attached to a component of a pattern. If the component matches, the matched substring is assigned as value to the name. This feature is called *value assignment in pattern matching.* A name is attached to a pattern component by using the binary value-assignment operator indicated by a period. For example

```
      NVOWEL    =    VOWEL . V
```

assigns to NVOWEL a pattern that matches a vowel (as given by VOWEL). The name V is attached to this pattern. Attaching a name to a pattern does not in any way affect what the pattern matches. However, if the pattern matches, the substring it matches is assigned to V. For example, if the value of WORD is BUSY, the statement

```
      WORD    NVOWEL
```

succeeds, and the string U is assigned to the name V. On the other hand, if the value of WORD is GYPSY, the statement fails. In this case, since no string is matched, no assignment is made to V. The value of V is unchanged, and remains whatever it was before the execution of the statement.

Names may be attached to components of patterns in as many places as desired. In this way the substrings matched by different components of the pattern can be determined. A simple example is

```
      DVOWEL    =    VOWEL . V1  VOWEL . V2
```

in which V1 is attached to the first vowel and V2 to the second. If DVOWEL matches, the individual vowels are assigned to V1 and V2.

Values are assigned to attached names only if the entire pattern matches. Thus if WORD is BUSY, the statement

```
        WORD    DVOWEL
```

fails. No assignment is made to V1, in spite of the fact that the first VOWEL matches, since the entire pattern does not match.

## 2.9 REPLACEMENT

Pattern matching makes it possible to examine the structure of a subject string and to transfer control depending on whether or not a pattern successfully matches. A combination of pattern matching and assignment, called *replacement*, makes it possible to modify, as well as to examine, the subject string. Replacement is indicated by following the pattern match with an equal sign and the value which is to replace the substring found by the pattern match:

*subject* *pattern* = *value*

As in assignment and pattern-matching statements, all components of the replacement statement are separated by blanks.

An example of a replacement statement is

```
        WORD    'A'    =    'E'
```

If the letter A is found in the value of WORD, it is replaced by the letter E, changing the value of WORD accordingly. If WORD does not contain an A, the pattern match fails, and the value of WORD is not changed. Thus if the value of WORD is BAT, the statement above changes the value of WORD to BET. If the value of WORD is BUT, however, the pattern match fails and no replacement is made. Pattern matching proceeds from left to right. When replacement is made, only the substring matched is replaced. Therefore if WORD contains more than one A, only the first (leftmost) A is replaced by an E. To replace all As by Es, the statement must be executed repeatedly as long as the pattern match succeeds. This can be accomplished by the use of a success goto to transfer control back to the statement itself:

```
LOOP    WORD    'A'    =    'E'                :S(LOOP)
```

If WORD originally contains six As, the statement labeled LOOP is successfully executed six times as the As are found and replaced. When LOOP is executed the seventh time, the pattern match fails and execution continues with the next statement after LOOP.

If the pattern in a replacement statement contains several alternatives, only the substring actually matched is replaced. For example, if

```
        TEXT    VOWEL   'T'    =    '*'
```

succeeds, one of the strings AT, ET, IT, OT, or UT is replaced by a star. Which substring is replaced depends on which one occurs first in TEXT. If the value of TEXT before replacement is

```
PUT IT ON YOUR LEFT FOOT
```

the value after replacement is:

```
P* IT ON YOUR LEFT FOOT
```

Sometimes it is useful to eliminate a substring that occurs in another string. A substring can be deleted by replacing it by the null string. For example, to remove all vowels from TEXT, the following statement could be used:

```
REMV    TEXT    VOWEL    =                         :S(REMV)
```

As in assignment statements, an omitted value in the replacement statement signifies the null string.

Replacement and value assignment may be used in combination. For example, the statement

```
        TEXT    LEN(1) . C    =
```

deletes a character from TEXT and assigns that character to C. This statement fails if the value of TEXT is the null string.

## 2.10 INPUT AND OUTPUT

The input and output of data performed by computer programs is often shrouded in mystery and regarded with some anxiety by beginning programmers. In SNOBOL4, input and output are quite simple, and need not be a cause for concern.

In the first place, it is necessary to understand why input and output are important and what they do. Data in one form or another is an important component of almost all programs. Some data may be contained in the program in the form of numbers and strings. Usually data is not part of a program itself, but is read in by the program for processing. Most programs, in fact, are designed so that they can be used on different sets of data as desired. An example is a program that computes the frequency with which letters occur in text. Such a program might be applied to many different examples of text. The text therefore cannot be part of the program itself.

Data may be organized in a variety of ways. Most typically, a line of information is called a *record* and a collection of records arranged in some order is called a *file*. These terms have their origin in business file systems which were in existence before the development of computers. The organization of data into records and files for processing by a program is more of a physical matter than a logical one. Each time the program requests data, it gets a record. In SNOBOL4, input records are fixed in length and usually correspond to 80-character punched cards. A file composed of records may consist of a deck of cards, or it may be stored on one of the many devices used to store such machine-readable data. Magnetic tapes and disks are most commonly used.

Input is requested in SNOBOL4 by using the name INPUT. INPUT is a variable like FIRST and SECOND, but it has the special property of fetching the next data record every time it is used. The record fetched becomes the value of INPUT. For example, in the statement

```
        CARD    =    INPUT
```

the use of INPUT causes a record to be read and assigned to CARD. In the SNOBOL4 program, this record becomes an 80-character string. Each time INPUT is used, a record is read and becomes the new value of INPUT. It is typical to assign the value of INPUT to another variable (such as CARD in the example above) to prevent the value from being lost on the next reference to INPUT.

Successive uses of INPUT result in the reading of successive records of the input file in the order in which they occur on that file. If reading continues, data in the file is eventually exhausted. When the end of the file is reached (often referred to as an end-of-file condition, or simply "end of file"), this fact is signaled to the program to prevent further attempts to read from the file. In SNOBOL4, an end of file causes failure of the statement in which INPUT was used. Therefore a statement that reads data should have a failure goto:

```
        CARD    =    INPUT                          :F(NODATA)
```

In this case, when the input file is exhausted, control is transferred to a statement with the label NODATA. Providing a failure exit on statements that do input is quite important since an attempt to read past the end of a file may have unpleasant effects. Exactly what may happen depends on the particular system on which SNOBOL4 is running, but in any event, such an "accident" should be avoided.

In order for a program to display the results of its calculations, it must perform output as well as input. The mechanism for output is similar to that for input. The name OUTPUT, like INPUT, also has a special meaning. Whenever OUTPUT is assigned a value, that value is printed. For example

```
        OUTPUT    =    SECOND
```

prints the value of SECOND as well as assigning it to OUTPUT. The value of OUTPUT is not transitory like that of INPUT, and OUTPUT can be used like any other variable except that whenever OUTPUT is assigned a value, that value is printed.

The ease of doing input and output is illustrated by the statement

```
        OUTPUT    =    INPUT                        :F(NODATA)
```

which reads a record, prints it, and leaves the value in OUTPUT for subsequent use.

Values assigned to OUTPUT are printed and may be read and kept for future reference. Such printed output is not in machine-readable form; i.e., it cannot be read back into the computer. Very often it is desirable to save computed data in a form that is machine-readable. This may be accomplished by punching the data on cards rather than by printing it. The name PUNCH is used for this purpose. The statement

```
        PUNCH    =    RESULT
```

assigns the value of RESULT to PUNCH and also causes a copy of the value to be punched on a card. Each assignment to PUNCH produces a new card. In fact, since the standard punched card is 80 characters long, if the value assigned to PUNCH is longer than 80 characters, additional cards are punched as necessary.

A null string assigned to OUTPUT causes a blank line to be printed. Similarly, a null string assigned to PUNCH causes a blank card to be punched.

A value assigned to OUTPUT or PUNCH as a result of value assignment in pattern matching also produces output. The following statement illustrates such a usage:

```
        LINE    LEN(20) . PUNCH    =
```

This statement removes the first 20 characters from LINE and punches them on a card. Of course, if the value of LINE is less than 20 characters long, the statement fails and no card is punched.

There are ways of directing output to other media, such as tape or disk. Use of these media generally varies from installation to installation and is not discussed here.

## 2.11 SOME SIMPLE PROGRAMS

The preceding sections describe the rudiments of the SNOBOL4 language. Before going on, it is worth seeing how the material already described can be put together to create some simple but complete programs. Consider the following problems:

1. Write a program which reads in a data file and counts the number of times the character S occurs in this file. Print out the file and the result of the calculation.
2. Modify Program 1 to count occurrences of any of the characters M, R, T, and W in addition to S.
3. Write a program to determine whether a data file contains an even or an odd number of commas.
4. Write a program to reverse strings of characters, end for end.

One of the greatest difficulties in learning any programming language is knowing where to begin. One can read about all kinds of features and yet not know how to *do* anything. An example is usually the easiest way to get started, and for that reason these four simple programs are worked out here in some detail.

**Program 1**

This program must read in data and print it out. Assume, therefore, that the data is on the input file (perhaps actually punched on cards). The simple statement

```
READ    OUTPUT   =    INPUT                    :S(READ)F(EOF)
```

will suffice to read and print the data. However each record must be processed. Therefore, before reading another record, the current record must be analyzed. A start is given by the two statements

```
READ    OUTPUT   =    INPUT                    :F(EOF)
        TEXT   =    OUTPUT
```

so that an input record is assigned to TEXT and may now be processed. The desired substring can be located by a pattern-matching statement such as:

```
        TEXT    'S'                            :S(YES)F(NO)
```

To count occurrences of S, a value, perhaps identified by the name COUNT, can be incremented. Thus the following two statements evolve:

```
AGAIN   TEXT    'S'                            :F(NO)
        COUNT   =    COUNT + 1                 :(AGAIN)
```

These lines contain a rather common mistake, and produce a bane of the programmer's existence: an endless loop. If TEXT does contain S, COUNT is incremented, but the same S is found the next time, and so on. An easy way to avoid such a loop is to remove S each time it is found. The statements become:

```
AGAIN   TEXT    'S'    =                       :F(NO)
        COUNT   =    COUNT + 1                 :(AGAIN)
```

Now there is no danger of looping, because every time S is found, it is removed. Eventually, TEXT will contain no more occurrences of S.

The next question is where to go if S is not found in TEXT. The label NO has been provided, but the next step in this case is to read another card, so the transfer should be to READ to get the next line for processing. A few things remain to complete the program. The initial value of COUNT should be set to zero before any data is read. Finally, when READ fails, the count must be printed out. The complete program is:

```
        COUNT    =  0

READ    OUTPUT    =   INPUT                               :F(EOF)

        TEXT   =    OUTPUT

AGAIN   TEXT   'S'     =                                  :F(READ)

        COUNT  =     COUNT + 1                            :(AGAIN)

EOF     OUTPUT  =

        OUTPUT  =     'THE TOTAL COUNT IS ' COUNT

END
```

A blank line is printed at EOF to separate the line containing the total count from the text which has already been printed. This is just a small extra touch to make the results easier to read. Program execution terminates when control flows into the END statement. Printed output resulting from running this program on a file consisting of two data records follows:

```
DATA STRINGS THAT APPEAR EXPLICITLY IN A PROGRAM ARE

DISTINGUISHED FROM NAMES BY ENCLOSING QUOTATION MARKS.


THE TOTAL COUNT IS 7
```

**Program 2**

Once Program 1 has been worked out, Program 2 follows naturally; only one line need be changed. Instead of one character, any one of five must be counted. This amounts to adding four alternatives to the pattern used in AGAIN:

```
AGAIN   TEXT   'S' | 'M' | 'R' | 'T' | 'W'   =      :F(READ)
```

A host of related programs can be provided in a similar manner. A more elegant way of providing for such generality is to assign the pattern to a variable at the beginning of the program and to use that variable in the pattern-matching statement. For Program 2 this might be done as follows:

```
        PAT     =   'S' | 'M' | 'R' | 'T' | 'W'

        COUNT   =    0

READ    .

        .

        .

AGAIN   TEXT    PAT     =                                 :F(READ)

        .

        .

        .
```

Now it is an easy matter to change PAT to count other things using the same program.

**Program 3**

Determining whether text contains an even or odd number of commas can be accomplished by counting the commas first. Counting commas may be done in the same fashion as counting the strings in Programs 1 and 2. Simply changing PAT to

```
        PAT     =   ','
```

takes care of the counting problem. It remains to determine whether the result is odd or even. This can be done by determining if the number of commas is evenly divisible by two. The built-in function REMDR can be used to perform this computation. That is, if REMDR(COUNT,2) is zero, the count is even. Otherwise it is odd. This may be tested by applying the predicate EQ :

```
EOF     EQ(REMDR(COUNT,2),0)                              :F(ODD)

        OUTPUT  =   'COUNT IS EVEN'                       :(END)

ODD     OUTPUT  =   'COUNT IS ODD'

END
```

Note the transfer to END to terminate program execution in the case that the number is even.

**Program 4**

Reversing a string is somewhat different from the preceding problems. First, the program must be able to reverse strings regardless of what characters they contain. Thus pattern matching for specific characters is not the way to approach the problem. A pattern constructed by LEN is therefore suggested. A string can be reversed by removing one character (LEN(1)) at a time and building up a new string one character at a time, but in the opposite order. If the string to be reversed is the value of TEXT, statements like the following could be used:

```
REM     TEXT     LEN(1) . C    =
        REVERSE     =    C REVERSE                        :(REM)
```

The first statement removes a character from the beginning of TEXT. The second statement places that character on the front of REVERSE. To see how the reversal proceeds, suppose the value of TEXT is XYZ. Successive executions of the statements above produce:

| TEXT | REVERSE |
|---|---|
| XYZ | |
| YZ | X |
| Z | YX |
| | ZYX |

Two things remain to assure that the program works properly. When the value of TEXT becomes null, the statement labeled REM will fail. To avoid an endless loop, a failure goto must be provided. Finally, if the statements are to be used on more than one string, REVERSE must be set to null before beginning. Otherwise, characters would be concatenated onto the last reversed string. The complete section of program is:

```
        REVERSE    =
REM     TEXT  LEN(1) . C    =                            :F(DONE)
        REVERSE  =   C REVERSE                           :(REM)
DONE    .
        .
        .
```

Incorporating these statements into a program that processes data on file and prints the results is left to the reader.

## 2.12 PROGRAM FORMAT

Most programs are punched on 80-column cards, using a keypunch machine. In any event, programs are prepared line by line. Usually one statement is written on each card. If a statement has a label, that label must begin at the beginning of the card, in column one. If a statement has no label, column one must be blank. The rest of the statement is punched as described in the preceding sections, with the components separated by blanks as required. The first 72 characters of a card can be used for the statement. The last eight characters are usually left blank but can be used for identification, such as sequence numbers, if desired. These eight characters are not part of the statement.

Sometimes a statement is too long to fit in the 72 columns available on a card. This may happen, for example, when a number of long data strings appear in the same statement. If a statement is too long to fit on one card, it may be continued on successive cards. To continue a statement, special rules must be followed. First, a statement can be divided between cards only where blanks are used for concatenation, to surround binary operators, or to separate components. Cards which continue a statement must have a + in column one. The following statement illustrates continuation.

```
        OUTPUT  =   'THE RESULTS OF THE SURVEY SHOW THAT '
+                   FINAL ' CUSTOMERS WERE SATISFIED'
```

A statement may be continued on as many lines as necessary. One precaution must be observed: a statement *cannot* be divided at a blank that occurs in a data string. If a data string is too long to fit on a line, it must be divided into two data strings that are then concatenated.

More than one statement can be placed on a single line if desired. In this case, a semicolon ends a statement and a new statement can be begun immediately following a semicolon. If the next statement begins with a label, that label must begin at the first character after the semicolon. An example of three statements written on one line is:

```
        I  =  1;   N  =  10;RETRY  COUNT  =  0
```

The third statement has a label, RETRY.

Lines that begin with a * are considered to be comments and are ignored when the program is run. Such lines may be used to insert descriptive information in the program. See Section 8.2.

The last statement of a program is an end statement containing the label END, which indicates the end of the program. If the program reads data, the data records immediately follow the end card. The program and data together make up a deck of cards which can then be run on a computer. See Appendices A and C for more information.

## EXERCISES

**2.1.** Identify all the integers, data strings, names, and labels in the solution given to Problem 1 in Section 2.11.

**2.2.** Determine the values assigned to names by the following statements:

```
I = 100

J = I * I

K = (I / 10) + 3

L = (K * I) + (K - 5)

WORD1 = 'COGITO'

WORD2 = 'ERGO'

WORD3 = 'SUM'

CLAUSE = WORD1 ' ' WORD2 ' ' WORD3

SENTENCE = CLAUSE '.'

ENDVOWEL = ('A' | 'E' | 'I' | 'O' | 'U') . V ' '

CLAUSE ENDVOWEL
```

**2.3.** Write patterns that match
(a) any single even digit.
(b) any punctuation mark.
(c) any vowel that is immediately followed by a punctuation mark.
(d) pairs of vowels separated by three characters.

**2.4.** A string that reads the same forward and backward is called a palindrome. An example is:

```
ABLE WAS I ERE I SAW ELBA
```

Write statements that determine if a string is a palindrome.

**2.5.** Write statements to rotate a string left N characters, where N is a positive integer. For example, the result of rotating the string mentioned in Exercise 2.4 by 3 positions is:

```
E WAS I ERE I SAW ELBAABL
```

**2.6.** Write a program that simply prints and punches a data file.

CHAPTER 3

# Numbers and Strings

SNOBOL4 is frequently used for problems involving strings of characters because of its facilities for handling string data. Almost every program also deals with numbers in some way. It may be necessary to count the number of times a statement is executed in a loop, to compare lengths of strings, or to compute averages, for example.

## 3.1 ARITHMETIC OPERATIONS

### Binary Operators

The most common arithmetic operations are addition, subtraction, multiplication, and division. Exponentiation, the raising of a number to a power (e.g. $2^3$), is less frequently used but is still familiar. The symbols for these binary operations in SNOBOL4 are

```
+   -   *   /   !
```

respectively. The pair of symbols `**` also may be used to indicate exponentiation.

These operators require two operands and, like all binary operators in SNOBOL4, they must be surrounded by blanks. The operands may be numbers, names that have numerical values, or, in fact, any expressions that have numerical values. For example, the statements

```
N     =    10

M     =    N + 3
```

assign the values 10 and 13 to N and M respectively. Consider the expression:

```
M * 3 + 2
```

At first glance, this may not appear to be a valid expression, since every binary operator requires two operands and in the expression above there are two operators but only three operands. Actually, the result of one binary operation provides an operand for the other. The expression above is equivalent to

```
(M * 3) + 2
```

where parentheses indicate grouping of the parts of the expression. Thus the expression `M * 3` is the left operand of the `+`. The next question is: Why are the parentheses placed where they are shown above? The other choice would be:

```
M * (3 + 2)
```

Note that this grouping would give a different value. The first grouping is correct and was not chosen arbitrarily or because the `*` comes first. The reason is that multiplication has higher *precedence* than addition. Precedence determines how tightly an operator binds to its operands. In the expression above, the middle operand, `3`, is contended for by the two operators `*` and `+`. Since `*` has higher precedence than `+`, `*` gets the operand. While precedence of operators is largely a matter of mathematical convention, not all programming languages have the same rules of precedence. In SNOBOL4 the precedence of the binary arithmetic operators in order from highest to lowest is:

```
!

*

/

+ -
```

Addition and subtraction have the same precedence, as indicated. Using the relative precedences given above, the expression

```
N ! 2 * 3 + M
```

is grouped as:

```
((N ! 2) * 3) + M
```

Parentheses can be used as desired to make the groupings more evident or to group terms in a different way than would be implied by precedence. An example is

```
(N + 2) * (M + 3)
```

which would have a different meaning if the parentheses were removed.

Precedence does not solve all the problems of grouping operands and operators. Consider the following expression.

```
A - B - C
```

There are two possible groupings

```
(A - B) - C
```

and

```
A - (B - C)
```

In the first, the operators *associate* to the left, while in the second they associate to the right. Association, like precedence, is partly a matter of convention, but it depends on the properties of the operators. The first choice above is correct since subtraction associates to the left. In fact, all binary operators associate to the left except exponentiation. In mathematical notation,

$$a^{b^c} \quad \text{means} \quad a^{(b^c)}$$

In SNOBOL4, the equivalent expression

```
A ! B ! C
```

is grouped as:

```
A ! (B ! C)
```

There are other binary operators than the arithmetic ones; concatenation and alternation are examples. Appendix B contains a table of all binary operators with their precedence and associativity.

### Unary Operators

There are two unary arithmetic operators that have only a single operand. These are + and -. The unary - changes the sign of a number. For example, if the value of M is 13,

```
P    =    -M
```

assigns the value -13 to P. Note that there is no blank between the unary operator and its operand. This distinguishes unary operators from binary operators. The unary + operator does not change the numerical value of its operand. That is, the values 5 and +5 are the same. The + is included for completeness to complement the unary - operator.

Unary operators have the highest possible precedence and are always grouped with the operand to their right. Thus the expression

```
-A * B
```

is equivalent to:

```
(-A) * B
```

### Numerical Predicates

There are six numerical predicates for comparing the value of numbers. They are

| | |
|---|---|
| EQ | equal to |
| GE | greater than or equal to |
| GT | greater than |
| LE | less than or equal to |
| LT | less than |
| NE | not equal to |

For example

```
GT(3,5)
```

fails, but

```
NE(3,5)
```

succeeds. As is the case with all functions, the arguments of these predicates may be expressions. Thus

```
EQ(M + N,SIZE(S))
```

succeeds if the sum of M and N is equal to the number of characters in the value of S.

## 3.2 INTEGER ARITHMETIC

Integers are whole numbers which may be positive, negative, or zero. The result of arithmetic operations on integers is generally what would be expected, as is illustrated by examples throughout this book. There are a few cases, however, in which arithmetic performed by a programming language may produce different results from those which might be expected.

In the first place, there is a limit to how large an integer value may be. This limit depends somewhat on the particular computer that is used. On a typical computer, the limit is about 2,000,000,000. This may seem like such a large number that the limit can be ignored, but some types of computation produce very large numbers quite quickly, and the existence of a limit should be remembered.

Division of integers is a real problem Consider the statement:

```
Q    =    I / 2
```

If the value of I is 4, the value assigned to Q is 2. Suppose the value of I is 3. In long-hand computation, the result of such an operation is usually written as 3/2 or 1 1/2. Since 2 does not divide 3 evenly, a fraction results. SNOBOL4, however, does not produce fractions. The result of an operation on integers is an integer. The fractional part is simply discarded. Thus, the value assigned to Q in the statement above is 1. Discarding the fractional part is called *truncation.* Integer division in SNOBOL4 always truncates the result. This may produce quite unexpected results in some cases.

For example, the value of

```
2 * (1 / 2)
```

is 0. Recall, however, that the built-in function REMDR computes the remainder resulting from integer division: that is, the part discarded by truncation. Thus if the value of I is 3,

```
R     =     REMDR(I,2)
```

assigns 1 to R.

## 3.3 REAL NUMBERS

Integers are adequate for most numerical computations. There are some problems, however, that cannot be handled conveniently with integers. Consider the problem of computing an average. Suppose that grades on an examination are 75, 91, 83, 65, 84, and 93. The average of these six grades is:

$$\frac{75+91+83+65+84+93}{6}$$

The sum of the grades could be obtained by:

```
SUM     =     75 + 91 + 83 + 65 + 84 + 93
```

which assigns 491 to SUM, If SUM is divided by 6, the result is 81 with a remainder of 5. This is illustrated by the statements:

```
Q     =     SUM / 6

R     =     REMDR(SUM,6)
```

which assign 81 and 5 to Q and R respectively. Thus the average is 81 + 5/6. In long hand, such computations are usually performed in decimal form, however, and the average represented as 81.8333... or, discarding the less significant digits, simply 81.83.

SNOBOL4 provides *real numbers* for performing such computations. Real numbers are represented with decimal points. Consider the statement:

```
Q     =     I / 2.0
```

The divisor 2.0 is a real number as indicated by the decimal point. If the value of I is 3.0, the value assigned to Q is 1.5.

Real numbers have several advantages over integers. In the first place, there is no truncation as a result of division, so that the result of executing

```
Q    =    (75.0 + 91.0 + 83.0 + 65.0 + 84.0 + 93.0) / 6.0
```

is 81.8333. Another advantage is that very large values can be represented using real numbers. On a typical computer, the largest real number is approximately 1,000,000, 000,000,000,000,000,000,000,000,000,000,000,000,000,000,000,000,000,000,000,000, 000,000,000—which is large enough for most of us! Very tiny fractions can be represented also.

The numerical predicates described in Section 3.1 can be used for comparing real numbers as well as integers.

## 3.4 MIXED MODE ARITHMETIC

The previous sections have illustrated computations with two types of numbers: integers and real numbers. What happens if both types occur in the same arithmetic expression? The answer is quite simple: If an arithmetic expression contains a real number, the result of the entire expression is a real number. This is illustrated by:

```
Q    =    (75 + 91 + 83 + 65 + 84 + 93) / 6.0
```

the result is 81.8333 as before. To be more specific, the sum in parentheses is computed first. Since all numbers in the sum are integers, the result is 491, an integer. Next the division is performed. The operation is equivalent to:

```
Q    =    491 / 6.0
```

Since this expression contains a real number, the result is a real number (81.8333).

Numerical predicates can also be used for comparing real numbers to integers.

## 3.5 STRING-VALUED FUNCTIONS

### Trimming Strings

Strings sometimes have unneeded or unwanted blanks at the end. Typically this happens when data is read in, since the value assigned to INPUT corresponds to an 80-character card. If only a few characters are punched on a card, the remaining (trailing) characters are blanks. The function TRIM removes trailing blanks.

```
T    =    TRIM(S)
```

assigns to T a string which is the same as the value of S, except that trailing blanks are omitted. If S does not end with a blank, T and S are the same. TRIM(S) does not change the value of S in any way; it simply returns a value that is a function of the value of S. To actually trim blanks from the value of S, the following statement may be used.

```
          S       =       TRIM(S)
```

Since the trailing blanks that result from reading data are often unnecessary, TRIM may be applied to all references to INPUT. A typical statement is:

```
READ      LINE    =       TRIM(INPUT)                     :F(EOF)
```

Trimming of all input records can be done in a simpler way by using the keyword &TRIM. Ordinarily the value of &TRIM is zero, in which case records are read in with trailing blanks. If the value of &TRIM is set to a positive integer, however, all trailing blanks are automatically removed on input. A program in which trailing blanks on input are not wanted might therefore start with the statement:

```
          &TRIM   =       1
```

Then the statement

```
READ      LINE    =       INPUT                           :F(EOF)
```

could be used.

### Duplicating Strings

Sometimes it is useful to concatenate several copies of the same string. For example, a string of 80 dashes might be used to draw a line on the output listing to separate two sets of results. A string of 80 dashes can be obtained by repeated concatenation, but that is awkward and time consuming. The function DUPL performs this type of operation directly. The value of DUPL(S,N) is the string S duplicated N times. The line described above would be printed by the single statement:

```
          OUTPUT  =       DUPL('-',80)
```

The first argument of DUPL need not be a one-character string; it may be any string. The value of DUPL('-*',6) is:

```
-*-*-*-*-*-*
```

### Character Replacement

Pattern matching provides facilities for locating and replacing strings of characters. Sometimes only single characters need to be replaced. While this may be done by executing replacement statements repeatedly, the process is awkward and time consuming. For replacement of individual characters by other characters, the built-in function REPLACE is more useful. REPLACE has three arguments. The first is the string on which the replacement is to be performed. The second and third arguments are strings that describe the characters to be replaced and what these characters are to be replaced by, respectively. A simple example is provided by the statement

```
        RTEXT    =    REPLACE(TEXT,'A','*')
```

which replaces every A by a * in the value of TEXT and assigns the result to RTEXT. If the value of TEXT is

```
ADVANCED METHODS APPLY
```

the resulting value of RTEXT is

```
*DV*NCED METHODS *PPLY
```

Only As are replaced; the other characters are unchanged.

More than one character can be replaced at a time. To replace all vowels by *s, the following statement could be used:

```
        RTEXT    =    REPLACE(TEXT,'AEIOU','*****')
```

For the data given above, the value of RTEXT is:

```
*DV*NC*D M*TH*DS *PPLY
```

In the second and third arguments, character replacement is specified by the position of corresponding characters. Thus the statement

```
        RTEXT    =    REPLACE(TEXT,'AEIOU','*$-&/')
```

gives RTEXT the value:

```
*DV*NC$D M$TH&DS *PPLY
```

Since neither I nor U occur in TEXT, the corresponding characters - and / do not appear in the result. The one-to-one correspondence between characters in the second and third arguments of REPLACE is illustrated diagramatically in Figure 3.1.

```
A  E  I  O  U
↓  ↓  ↓  ↓  ↓
*  $  -  &  /
```

**Figure 3.1** Correspondence of Character Sets in REPLACE

One useful feature of REPLACE is that characters can be simultaneously interchanged. An example is illustrated by the statement:

```
        ITEXT    =    REPLACE(RTEXT,'*$','$*')
```

If RTEXT has the value given in the previous example, the value assigned ITEXT is:

```
$DV$NC*D M*TH&DS $PPLY
```

The lengths of the second and third arguments of REPLACE must be the same. If they are not, REPLACE fails without returning a value. While it is meaningful for the same character to appear in the third argument more than once, a character that appears in the second argument more than once specifies two, possibly different, replacements. In this case the last (right-most) specification is used.

## 3.6 INDIRECT REFERENCING

Data strings that appear explicitly in a program are distinguished from names by enclosing quotation marks. For example in the statement

```
FRENCH    =    'ROMANCE'
```

ROMANCE is a data string. FRENCH is also a string, but it is used as a name, not as data. Yet in the statement

```
LANGUAGE    =    'FRENCH'
```

FRENCH is used as a data string.

In SNOBOL4, these two uses of a string are related. Figure 3.2 illustrates this relationship using arrows to point from names to their values.

LANGUAGE → FRENCH → ROMANCE

**Figure 3.2** Strings as Names and Data

A name is often used to reference its value. A simple example is

```
OUTPUT    =    LANGUAGE
```

which prints FRENCH. SNOBOL4 has an indirect-referencing operation which references the value of a value. This operation is indicated by the unary operator $ written in front of the name to be indirectly referenced. An example is

```
OUTPUT    =    $LANGUAGE
```

which prints ROMANCE: that is, the value of the value of LANGUAGE.

Indirect referencing may be perplexing at first, and the source of some confusion. One way to think of indirect referencing is as an application of an arrow, like that shown in Figure 3.2, that moves from a name to its value.

Indirect referencing makes it natural to use a name to represent data (for example FRENCH to represent the French language). In a similar way, a value may be assigned to a name to represent an attribute which that name has (French is a Romance language). A name may have various values at different times, depending on the data under consideration. Thus the value of LANGUAGE might be FRENCH at one time and GERMAN at another. In either case, the value of $LANGUAGE would be the type of language currently under consideration.

Values may also be assigned using indirect referencing. Thus if the value of LANGUAGE is SPANISH, the statement

```
      $LANGUAGE     =     'ROMANCE'
```

assigns the value ROMANCE to SPANISH. This feature is particularly useful when one wants to use a name that contains characters that are not allowed in name. For example, suppose that the compound word SERBO-CROATIAN is to be given a value. The statement

```
      SERBO-CROATIAN     =     'SLAVIC'
```

is erroneous since a dash cannot be used in name. However, the following statement is legal and accomplishes the desired result:

```
      $'SERBO-CROATION'     =     'SLAVIC'
```

Here indirect referencing is applied directly to a data string so that a value may be assigned to it. Any nonnull string can be assigned a value in this way.

More than one level of indirect referencing may be used. Suppose the following statements are executed:

```
      TOPIC     =   'LANGUAGE'

      LANGUAGE   =     'SPANISH'
```

Then the statement

```
      $$TOPIC    =     'ROMANCE'
```

assigns the value ROMANCE to the name SPANISH.

There is no limit to the number of levels of indirect referencing that may be used, but potential confusion is a limiting factor in practice.

In the examples above, indirect referencing is used to associate data using name-value relationships. Indirect referencing may also be used in gotos. For example, if the value of PROCESS is PARSE, the goto :($PROCESS) transfers control to PARSE. For other values of PROCESS, control is transferred to other labeled statements. Such a "computed goto" serves as a switch to select an appropriate statement. The statement selected by an indirect goto can even be specified by data read into the program. For example, the statement

```
      LABEL     =     TRIM(INPUT)                          :S($LABEL)F(EOF)
```

transfers to a label given on a data card.

## 3.7 COMPARING STRINGS

Although the predicate IDENT may be used to determine whether or not any two objects are identical, IDENT is most commonly used to compare two strings. Two strings are identical if they are the same, character by character. The way the strings are created is irrelevant. Thus

```
IDENT(DUPL('A',3),'AAA')
```

succeeds even though one argument is the value of a function and the other is given literally.

Strings may be compared lexically, that is alphabetically, by using the predicate LGT ("lexically greater than"). For example

```
OUTPUT   =   LGT(ITEM,LAST) ITEM
```

prints the value of ITEM, provided the value of ITEM is lexically greater than the value of LAST. A string is lexically greater than another if it would follow that string in an alphabetical list. Thus TO is greater than SOUTH, and TOP is greater than TO. The null string is lexically less than any other string.

The order of letters in determining lexical order is the standard one, but strings compared by LGT may contain characters other than letters. The position of other characters varies from one type of computer to another. For example, on some computers the digits come before the letters, while on others the digits come after the letters. The order of special characters is even more variable. As is mentioned in Chapter 2, not all computers provide the same characters or even the same number of characters. The set of all characters and their position for the purpose of determining lexical order is the value of &ALPHABET. For example, to determine the available characters, the following statement might be used.

```
OUTPUT   =   &ALPHABET
```

&ALPHABET is a protected keyword. Its value cannot be changed by an assignment and therefore the character set is always available for examination and use.

## 3.8 NUMBERS AND STRINGS

Consider the following statement

```
N   =   'A' * 3
```

This is surely a curious construction, since one of the operands of * is the string A. Arithmetic operations simply have no meaning unless their operands are numbers, and hence the statement above is erroneous. But now consider the statement:

```
N   =   '5' * 3
```

Again one of the operands is a string, but this time that string looks like a number. SNOBOL4 permits strings to be used in arithmetic expressions, provided those strings represent numbers. Strings that represent numbers are called *numeral strings*. Numeral strings may represent integers or real numbers and may have a sign. Thus the statement

```
P     =     36 / '-1.2'
```

assigns the real number -30.0 to P.

The fact that numeral strings are permitted in arithmetic operations is very useful since so many SNOBOL4 operations generate strings. Suppose, for example, that a data card has the number 385 punched on it. Then

```
LIMIT     =     TRIM(INPUT)
```

reads this card, discards trailing blanks, and assigns the *string* 385 to the name LIMIT. Even though the value of LIMIT is a string, it can be used in arithmetic expressions as an integer.

In numerical contexts, the null string is equivalent to the integer 0. This fact is useful since strings initially have null values which are numerically equivalent to zero. Similarly

```
GT(M)
```

succeeds if M is greater than zero, since the omitted second argument is null and hence equivalent to zero.

Just as numeral strings can be used in contexts that require numbers, so can numbers be used in contexts that require strings. For example, the statements

```
WORD      =     'FENESTRATION'

INDEX     =     'X' SIZE(WORD)
```

assign the string X12 to INDEX. SIZE(WORD) returns the integer 12 which is automatically converted to a string and concatenated with X.

Similarly, numbers can be printed and punched just as if they were strings. The statement

```
PUNCH     =     SIZE(WORD) / 2.0
```

punches 6.0 on a card.

Both concatenation and arithmetic may occur in the same expression. Concatenation, as a binary operator, has lower precedence than any of the arithmetic operators, and associates to the left. Thus the statement

```
OFFSET    =     'X' SIZE(WORD) + 3 'Y' SIZE(WORD) - 3
```

assigns X15Y9 to OFFSET.

Generally speaking, numbers and numeral strings can be used interchangeably without concern. There are a few situations in which the distinction between numbers and numeral strings is important. The predicate IDENT, for example, succeeds only if its two arguments are identical. Thus

```
IDENT('3',3)
```

fails. Therefore numerical predicates should be used for comparing numbers. For instance

```
EQ('3',3)
```

succeeds.

## EXERCISES

**3.1.** Insert parentheses in the following expressions to illustrate the grouping of terms according to the precedence and associativity of operators. Compute the value of each.

```
3 / 2 + 5 * 6

3 / 2 * 6

3 * 2 / 6

2.0 + 0 / 3 - 6.7

'7' * '3.5' / REMDR(5,7)

SIZE(DUPL('**',3)) * 2.0 + REMDR(31,100)

3 5 + 21

REMDR(37,15) REMDR(15,37) * 2
```

**3.2.** Write a program that reads grades punched on cards and computes the average grade. Assume that a single grade is punched left justified (starting in column one) on each card.

**3.3.** Write a program that prints an *n* by *m* matrix of dots. For example, if *n* is 3 and *m* is 5, the output should be

```
...
...
...
...
...
```

Assume *n* and *m* are given on two consecutive data cards.

**3.4.** Write a program to print a table of the squares of the integers from 1 to 25. Print one integer and its square on each line. Arrange the table so that the right-most digit of each integer is printed in character position 10 of the line and the right-most digit of its square is printed in position 20.

**3.5.** Write a program to "encode" strings by replacing each A by Z, each B by Y, and C by X and so forth. Read text to be encoded from data cards and print out the result.

**3.6.** If the value of NOUN is NOUN, what is the value of $NOUN? Of $$NOUN?

**3.7.** Write statements that read in words punched on cards. Use indirect referencing to assign to each word its length. Assume that each card contains a single word, left justified. If words read in are HAT, CLAPTRAP, and PERSIMMON, what values are assigned to these words?

CHAPTER 4

# Pattern Matching

Pattern matching is a large and important part of the SNOBOL4 language. Pattern matching has two distinct components: the construction of patterns, and the matching process itself, in which a string is examined to see if it is matched by a pattern. Although patterns must be constructed before they can be used in pattern matching, it is necessary to understand the matching process in order to know how to construct patterns. The first part of this chapter describes the matching process. The second part describes ways of constructing patterns.

## 4.1 THE PATTERN-MATCHING PROCESS

Pattern matching is basically a left-to-right examination of the subject string in which an attempt is made to match a construction specified by the pattern. For example, in the statement

```
        TEXT     'A'     =     '*'
```

the value of text is examined starting at the first (left-most) character for the substring A. If A is found, it is replaced by a *. If A is not found, examination continues with the second character and so on. Thus if the value of TEXT initially is

```
ALWAYS STRIVE
```

the new value is:

```
*LWAYS STRIVE
```

If the pattern is E instead of A, the result is:

```
ALWAYS STRIV*
```

In this case, attempts to match the pattern E at the first twelve character positions fail, but finally succeed at the thirteenth. Since pattern matching works from left to right, examining successive characters of the subject string, it is convenient to assign numbers to the characters starting at the left. Thus W is the 3rd character in the string above. The position where pattern matching is focused at any time is called the *cursor position*. The cursor is an imaginary marker positioned after the last character examined. Initially, the cursor position is zero, which is before the first character of the string. In diagrams, the cursor position is indicated by an arrow, as illustrated below.

```
ALWAYS STRIVE
↑
```

Consider again the statement:

```
        TEXT   'E'   =    '*'
```

Successive cursor positions are:

```
ALWAYS STRIVE
↑

ALWAYS STRIVE
 ↑

ALWAYS STRIVE
  ↑

      •

      •

      •

ALWAYS STRIVE
           ↑

ALWAYS STRIVE
            ↑
```

Finally, when the cursor position is 12, the pattern E matches. The final situation is:

```
ALWAYS STRIVE
             ↑
```

The underline shows the substring matched by the pattern. It is this substring that is replaced by the *.

The process is exactly the same if the pattern is a longer string. For example, the statement

```
        TEXT    'WAYS'    =
```

results in the match

ALWAYS STRIVE

and the replacement produces AL STRIVE.

Note that although the examples here contain words, pattern matching has nothing to do with words as such. Strings may contain words, but pattern matching only deals with strings, and strings may contain any characters. All characters are equivalent in pattern matching; none has special significance.

Now suppose that instead of looking for a single string, one of several alternatives is sought. If VOWEL is a pattern constructed by the statement

```
        VOWEL    =    'A'  |  'E'  |  'I'  |  'O'  |  'U'
```

then the statement

```
LOOP    TEXT    VOWEL    =    '*'                          :S(LOOP)
```

might be used to mark the location of each VOWEL in TEXT.

In this case, at each cursor position a match is attempted for each of the alternatives in order from left to right as they appear in the pattern. If the value of TEXT is

STRIKE AT NOON

none of the alternatives matches at cursor positions 0, 1, or 2. However, at cursor position 3, the third alternative, I, matches:

STRIKE AT NOON

Since the pattern match succeeds, the value of text becomes:

STR*KE AT NOON

Executing the statement again, the vowel E is found when the cursor is at position 5. The replacement produces:

STR*K* AT NOON

Three more executions of the statement produce:

STR*K* *T N**N

This example has been drawn out somewhat to illustrate another point. Each time the statement is executed, pattern matching begins with the cursor at position zero.

Consequently there is much repetitive and time-consuming examination of the initial part of the string. Ways of avoiding such unnecessary examination are described in later sections.

Next consider a slightly more complicated situation. In the statement

```
          DVOWEL      =      VOWEL   VOWEL
```

DVOWEL consists of two components and is designed to match any two vowels in a row. In the spirit of the preceding example,

```
LOOP    TEXT    DVOWEL    =    '***'                      :S(LOOP)
```

might be used to mark occurrences of double vowels. Suppose the value of TEXT is:

```
TEACHERS LEAVE AT NOON
```

At cursor position zero, T is not matched by a vowel. However, at cursor position 1 the first component of DVOWEL matches E and the second component matches A. Thus the pattern match succeeds and replacement changes the value of TEXT to

```
T***CHERS LEAVE AT NOON
```

On the next execution, the first vowel is found and matched when the cursor position is 5. Thus the cursor is advanced to position 6:

```
T***CHERS LEAVE AT NOON
      ↑
```

R is not matched by the second component, however. Although the first component matches, the entire pattern does not. In this case, the pattern-matching process backs up and tries an alternative match for the previous component. Since no other alternative in this component matches at this position, the match for the first vowel is abandoned, and the cursor position is advanced, searching for a match farther along the string. At cursor position 10, another E is found and matched by the first component.

```
T***CHERS LEAVE AT NOON
           ↑
```

Now the second component matches the A and the pattern match succeeds.

The value of TEXT becomes:

```
T***CHERS L***VE AT NOON
```

A third execution of the statement results in:

```
T***CHERS L***VE AT N***N
```

The fourth execution fails. Note that in a pattern with several concatenated components, those components must match consecutive substrings. Although the string above still contains three substrings that are vowels, these substrings are not consecutive, and hence DVOWEL does not match.

### Anchored Matching

Ordinarily a pattern may match anywhere in the subject string, as illustrated by the examples in the preceding paragraphs. This mode of matching is called *unanchored* since the cursor is free to move down the subject string if that is necessary for the pattern to match. Pattern matching may be *anchored*, however, in which case the pattern must match a substring at the beginning of the subject string. In the anchored mode, a pattern match fails if the first component does not match with the cursor starting at position 0. Thus the statement

```
        TEXT    VOWEL
```

fails for the value of TEXT given above. Although TEXT contains vowels, it does not start with one.

The anchored mode is established by assigning a positive integer to the keyword &ANCHOR. Thus

```
        &ANCHOR    =    1
```

puts the anchored mode of pattern matching into effect. The initial value of &ANCHOR is 0, in which case pattern matching is unanchored. Any positive value establishes the anchored mode; the particular value is irrelevant.

The anchored mode may be turned on and off by changing the value of &ANCHOR. Usually one mode or the other will suffice for the entire program and the value of &ANCHOR may be assigned at the beginning of the program and left unchanged. The anchored mode of pattern matching should be used in situations where it is applicable since unnecessary attempts to match may be avoided.

## 4.2 CONSTRUCTION OF PATTERNS

The simplest patterns are strings. Alternation and concatenation permit the construction of more complicated patterns out of simpler ones. There are also a number of functions that return patterns as their values and a few built-in patterns that simply can be referred to by name.

### Positional Patterns

The patterns described so far match if the specified characters are found in the subject strings. There are also patterns that move the cursor, regardless of what characters occur in the subject string. Such patterns are constructed by functions. An example is the function LEN, described in Section 2.7. The argument of LEN specifies how far the cursor is to be moved.

Actually LEN is a function that returns a pattern as value. Thus the statement

```
        ONE    =    LEN(1)
```

assigns to ONE a pattern that matches any single character. Note that LEN does not *perform* pattern matching; it merely creates a pattern that can be used in pattern matching.

The argument of LEN may be any nonnegative integer. (The value of LEN(0) is a pattern that matches a null string.) Since patterns that are created by LEN merely move the cursor a specified number of positions to the right, they always match if the subject string is long enough.

TAB is another built-in function that creates a pattern which moves the cursor to the right. The pattern created by TAB moves the cursor to a specific position rather than a fixed distance. An example is given by the statement:

```
      TEXT    'C'    TAB(13) . T
```

If C is matched, the pattern created by TAB(13) moves the cursor to position 13, and the string between the C and position 13 is assigned to T. If the value of TEXT is

```
THEN THE CURTAIN FELL
```

the result is:

```
               T
              ___
THEN THE CURTAIN FELL
|<-----13----->|
```

The substring matched is CURT and the value assigned to T is URT.

The argument of TAB may be any nonnegative integer. During pattern matching, the resulting pattern simply moves the cursor right to the specified position. If that is not possible, the pattern fails to match. This may happen because the cursor is already beyond the specified position or because the subject string is not long enough. For example

```
      TEXT    'C'   TAB(2)
```

fails for the value of TEXT given above since the cursor is already at position 10 when the C is matched. Similarly

```
      TEXT    'C'   TAB(30)
```

fails because the subject string only contains 21 characters.

The built-in function RTAB is similar to TAB except that the position to which the cursor is moved is measured from the right end of the subject string. An example is given by:

```
      TEXT    'F'    RTAB(0) . RST
```

After F is matched, the cursor is moved to the right end of the string (i.e. zero characters from the end) as shown below.

```
                    RST
THEN THE CURTAIN FELL
                      ↑
```

The value assigned to RST is ELL.

Two built-in functions, POS and RPOS, create patterns that test the cursor position but do not move it. These patterns match if the cursor is in the specified position and fail otherwise. As in the case of TAB and RTAB, the cursor position is measured from the left and right respectively. An example is:

```
      TEXT    'N'  POS(4)
```

Since the cursor is at position 4 after N is matched, this pattern succeeds as illustrated.

```
THEN THE CURTAIN FELL
```

Notice that the pattern created by POS(4) does not move the cursor. Hence such patterns always match the null string.

A more interesting case is illustrated by:

```
      TEXT    'H'  POS(7)
```

The string H is matched as illustrated, but the pattern created by POS(7) fails since the cursor is in position 2, not position 7.

```
THEN THE CURTAIN FELL
```

Therefore the pattern-matching process backs up and attempts to find another match for the preceding component, H. Since this component is simply a string and has no alternatives, the matching process tries to find another H farther to the right. The successful result is illustrated below.

```
THEN THE CURTAIN FELL
```

The pattern above describes a situation requiring the string H to be found immediately before position 7. An equivalent pattern is given in the following statement.

```
      TEXT    POS(6)  'H'
```

RPOS is similar to POS except that the cursor position is measured from the right end of the subject string. In the statement

```
      TEXT    RPOS(1)  LEN(1) . LAST
```

the last character in the string is assigned to LAST.

### Character-Set Patterns

As is illustrated in the previous sections, specific strings can be given in patterns, and the cursor can be moved by positional patterns. There are also patterns that match any of a number of characters. These patterns are called *character-set patterns.*

One type of character-set pattern is constructed by the built-in function ANY. The argument of ANY may be any nonnull string of characters. The value of ANY is a pattern that matches any one of these characters. An example is:

```
        VWL     =     ANY('AEIOU')
```

VWL matches any one of the characters given in the argument: an A, E, I, O, or U. Thus VWL matches the same strings as the pattern VOWEL used in earlier examples. If there are many characters, ANY involves less writing than specifying each character as a separate alternative. It should be noted that while the argument of ANY is a string, i.e. a sequence of characters, these characters are all treated equally and their order is not important. Thus

```
        VWL     =     ANY('UOIEA')
```

is equivalent to the statement above.

The built-in function NOTANY constructs patterns that are the opposites of patterns matched by ANY. As a result

```
        NONVWL     =     NOTANY('AEIOU')
```

assigns to NONVWL a pattern that matches any single character that is *not* a vowel. NONVWL, for example, matches characters such as M, X, and $. Note that the effect of NOTANY can be achieved by using ANY and specifying all the characters that *are* to be matched. Since there are a large number of possible characters, it is sometimes simpler (as in the case above) to specify what is not to be matched than to specify what is to be matched.

ANY and NOTANY construct patterns that match single characters. There are two types of character-set patterns that can match longer strings. A pattern constructed by the built-in function SPAN matches the longest possible string consisting of consecutive characters given in its argument. An example is:

```
        VWLRUN     =     SPAN('AEIOU')
```

Unlike VWL, which matches a single vowel, VWLRUN matches a string of consecutive vowels. For example, if the value of TEXT is

```
HE YELLED "WHOOPIEEEE"
```

the statement

```
        TEXT     VWLRUN
```

would match E, the first string of vowels encountered matching from left to right:

```
HE YELLED "WHOOPIEEEE"
```

On the other hand, the statement

```
        TEXT     VWLRUN RPOS(1)
```

would match the string of vowels at the end:

```
HE YELLED "WHOOPIEEEE"
```

The built-in function BREAK constructs patterns that are, loosely speaking, opposites of patterns constructed by SPAN. An example is

```
        FINDVWL    =     BREAK('AEIOU')
```

which assigns to FINDVWL a pattern that matches any string of characters up to (but not including) a vowel. If the value of TEXT is that given in the preceding example, the statement

```
        TEXT     FINDVWL
```

simply matches the first H, moving the cursor up to the character E:

```
HE YELLED "WHOOPIEEEE"
 ↑
```

Note that the character E is not included in the substring that is matched. In order to match successfully, a pattern constructed by BREAK must find a character given in its argument. For example

```
        TEXT     BREAK('Z')
```

fails for the value of TEXT given above. On the other hand such a pattern may match the null string. An example is

```
        TEXT     BREAK('H')
```

which succeeds since H is the first character in the subject string, even though the cursor remains at position zero:

```
HE YELLED "WHOOPIEEEE"
↑
```

A pattern constructed by BREAK moves the cursor directly up to a character given in the argument. Therefore such a pattern may be used to avoid much of the repetitious matching that is required if the characters are specified using alternation. Consider the following statement:

```
FIND   TEXT   BREAK('AEIOU')  LEN(1) . V   =   :F(DONE)
```

This statement locates vowels, assigns them to V, and deletes both the vowel and the string of characters in front of it. Therefore subsequent examination of TEXT for vowels does not require useless re-examination of an initial string which contains no vowels. If the value of TEXT is

```
THEY ALL CONTRIBUTE
```

successive executions of the statement labeled FIND assign the vowels E, A, O, I, U, and E to V and change the value of TEXT as follows:

```
Y ALL CONTRIBUTE

LL CONTRIBUTE

NTRIBUTE

BUTE

TE
```

Finally the value of TEXT becomes null.

A use of BREAK and SPAN in conjunction is illustrated by the problem of matching words that appear in text. Words in text are separated by blanks, periods, and other punctuation marks. Although a general description of a word is quite complicated, for most purposes it is adequate to think of a word as a string of consecutive letters. Thus a pattern to match words might be:

```
        LETTER  =  'ABCDEFGHIJKLMNOPQRSTUVWXYZ'

        WPAT    =  SPAN(LETTER)
```

To remove successive words from a string of text and assign them to a name, a slightly more complicated pattern is needed.

```
        WPAT    =  BREAK(LETTER) SPAN(LETTER) . WORD
```

This pattern might be used in a statement such as:

```
GETW    TEXT    WPAT    =                               :F(NONE)
```

Each time this statement is executed, the first span of letters in TEXT is assigned to WORD. Any other characters before the first word are removed also. For example, if the value of TEXT is

```
WE KNOW HIM, OF COURSE.
```

then successive executions of GETW produce the words WE, KNOW, HIM, OF, and COURSE. TEXT is changed as follows:

```
WE KNOW HIM, OF COURSE.

 KNOW HIM, OF COURSE.

 HIM, OF COURSE.

, OF COURSE.

 COURSE.

.
```

Finally the value of TEXT becomes a single period and the pattern match fails.

### Built-in Patterns

The patterns described in the preceding sections were constructed by built-in functions, and depend on arguments supplied to these functions. There are a few patterns that are, themselves, built-in. These patterns are the initial values of certain names.

One such name is ARB whose initial value is a pattern that matches any string of arbitrary length or contents. Such a pattern may sound too general to be interesting. Patterns in the preceding sections provide for the matching of substrings of specified length containing unknown characters. In addition they provide for the matching of strings of known characters, but of unknown length. Sometimes, however, it is necessary to find the substring separating two specific substrings such as S and ING. The following pattern uses ARB to specify this situation.

```
      GAP    =    'S'   ARB . G   'ING'
```

Consider the statement:

```
      TEXT    GAP
```

If the value of TEXT is

```
WE ARE STARTING SOON
```

the pattern match succeeds and the substring TART is assigned to G:

```
          G
        ┌─^─┐
WE ARE STARTING SOON
       ‾‾‾‾‾‾‾‾
```

If the value of TEXT is

```
SING ALONG
```

the pattern also matches, and the null string is assigned to G:

```
SING ALONG
‾‾‾‾
```

Thus, ARB matches the string between S and ING in both cases. In the first case, this string is four characters long. In the second, it is zero characters long.

Another useful built-in pattern is REM which simply moves the cursor to the right end of the string and hence matches the remainder of the string. An example is given by:

```
        TEXT    'L'    REM . RST
```

For the value of TEXT shown above, this pattern matches and assigns ONG to RST:

```
        RST
        ┌─^─┐
SING ALONG
```

REM is identical to RTAB(0), and is included as a built-in pattern for convenience.

The built-in pattern BAL is somewhat more specialized than the two preceding patterns. BAL is designed for dealing with mathematical expressions. Such expressions often contain parentheses for grouping terms in the same way that SNOBOL4 does. A typical mathematical expression is:

```
(A+B)*(A-B)
```

A more complicated expression is:

```
((A+B)*(A-B)/(2+SIN(X)))
```

The second example illustrates nested components. Left and right parentheses are paired, and separating such an expression into its proper components involves locating the matching parentheses. In the expression above, some of the components are:

```
        (A+B)

        (A-B)

        (2+SIN(X))
```

The built-in pattern BAL matches strings that are balanced with respect to parentheses. The strings above are all balanced. A string which contains no parentheses at all is also balanced, but the null string is not considered to be balanced. It is an easy matter to determine if a string is balanced. Start at the left with a count of zero, add one for each left parenthesis, and subtract one for each right parenthesis. When the count reaches zero, the parentheses are balanced. This is illustrated by counting parentheses in the expression given below.

```
((A+B)*(A-B)/(2+SIN(X)))
12   1 2   1 2     3 210
```

If the count ever becomes negative, the expression is not balanced. Thus

```
)(A+B)*(A-B)/(2+SIN(X))(
```

is not balanced, although it contains an equal number of left and right parentheses.

BAL uses these rules to match balanced strings. For example, the statement

```
        MULOP     =     BAL . L '*' BAL . R
```

might be used to find two balanced expressions separated by a *.

If the value of FORMULA is

```
((A+B)*(A-B)/(2+SIN(X)))
```

the statement

```
        FORMULA    MULOP
```

succeeds and assigns (A+B) to L and (A-B) to R:

```
    L     R
 ┌──^──┐ ┌──^──┐
((A+B)*(A-B)/(2+SIN(X)))
```

Note that the matched substring begins with the second character of the subject string, since there are not two balanced strings separated by a * beginning with the first character.

BAL will match strings that do not contain any parentheses at all. Consider the pattern

```
        ADDOP     =     BAL . L '+' BAL . R
```

which is similar to MULOP, but with a different separating operator. If the value of FORMULA is as given above, the statement

```
        FORMULA    ADDOP
```

succeeds. A is assigned to L and B is assigned to R.

```
  L R
  ^ ^
((A+B)*(A-B)/(2+SIN(X)))
```

If a string contains no parentheses, BAL matches the shortest nonnull string that will satisfy the rest of the pattern. Thus if the value of FORMULA is

```
((V1*V2)-V3)+V4
```

The statement

```
        FORMULA    ADDOP
```

succeeds with L and R matching as shown.

```
     L          R
┌────^─────┐    ^
((V1*V2)-V3)+V4
```

However if ADDOP is changed to

```
          ADDOP     =     BAL . L '+' BAL . R RPOS(0)
```

the result is

```
       L           R
 ┌─────^─────┐   ┌^┐
((V1*V2)-V3)+V4
```

since RPOS(0) requires the second BAL to match the remainder of the string.

## 4.3 UNEVALUATED EXPRESSIONS

The beginning of this chapter stressed the point that pattern construction and pattern matching are two distinct operations. This is true even if the pattern is written out explicitly in the statement in which it is used for matching. In a statement such as

```
          TEXT     BREAK('H')
```

the built-in function BREAK is called and constructs a pattern. This pattern is *then* used in pattern matching. The two statements

```
          FINDH    =    BREAK('H')

          TEXT    FINDH
```

do the same thing, although the two steps make the two operations more obvious.

Quite often, patterns are constructed early in program execution, assigned to names, and then referred to by these names when needed in pattern matching. One advantage of this technique is that the patterns need only be constructed once, whereas if a pattern is written out explicitly in the statement in which it is used, it is reconstructed by SNOBOL4 each time that statement is executed. This is very wasteful if the matching statement is executed many times.

When patterns are constructed, names are often used to provide required values. Consider the simple problem of deleting the first N characters of a string. A statement to do this is:

```
REMOVE STRING    LEN(N)    =
```

The name N is used to provide the desired value of the argument of LEN. The pattern is constructed each time the statement is executed, and the number of characters removed depends on the value of N when the statement is executed. To avoid repetitious construction of the pattern, it is tempting to create a pattern at the beginning of the program, perhaps

```
          REMN     =     LEN(N)
```

and change the statement labeled REMOVE to be:

```
REMOVE STRING    REMN    =
```

Even if the value of N changes, the string matched by REMN does not. The value of N when REMN was created is part of that pattern and REMN does not change, regardless of subsequent changes in N.

To overcome problems such as this, evaluation of components in a pattern may be deferred until pattern matching takes place. This is done by using the unevaluated expression operator, the unary *. This operator prevents evaluation of its operand until that value is required during pattern matching. In the example above, the problem was the value of the name N. Therefore, if this value is not evaluated until needed during pattern matching, the pattern works as intended. The new pattern is:

```
        REMN    =    LEN(*N)
```

When this pattern is used in REMOVE, N is evaluated each time pattern matching is performed. Since the value of N is changing, the specified cursor position changes accordingly.

The unevaluated expression operator may be applied to the argument of any pattern-valued function: ANY, BREAK, LEN, NOTANY, POS, RPOS, RTAB, SPAN, or TAB. The unevaluated expression operator may not be applied to arguments of other built-in functions, but it may be applied to the operands of alternation and concatenation or an entire pattern. An example of a more complicated use of unevaluated expressions is:

```
        BLBK    =    *DUPL(' ',N) LEN(*N) . K
```

This pattern matches N blanks and assigns the next N characters to the name K. N is evaluated when BLBK is used in pattern matching. The use of DUPL(' ',*N) would be incorrect since the unevaluated expression operator can be applied only to arguments of pattern-valued functions. On the other hand, either of the two following statements would be correct and would match the same strings.

```
        BLBK    =    *(DUPL(' ',N) LEN(N) . K)

        BLBK    =    *DUPL(' ',N) *LEN(N) . K
```

## 4.4 ASSIGNMENT DURING PATTERN MATCHING

Names attached to components of patterns result in assignment of matched substrings to the attached names *if* the entire pattern match succeeds. These assignments are not performed until pattern matching is complete. Another type of attachment provides for *immediate assignment* when a component matches and does not depend on the success of the entire pattern match. A name is attached for immediate assignment by using the binary operator $.

An example is illustrated by the statements:

```
        TVOWEL    =    VOWEL $ V  'T'

        TEXT    TVOWEL
```

Suppose the value of TEXT is HELP. VOWEL matches the E, and at this point E is assigned to V. The T does not match, however, and since there are no more vowels in the string, the pattern match fails. Nevertheless, E has been assigned to V. Suppose the value of TEXT is:

HELPING HANDS

VOWEL first matches E, which is assigned to V. Since the next character is not a T, another match is attempted for VOWEL. Eventually I is found and assigned to V. Once again the next character is not a T, so a search for another vowel is made. Finally A is assigned to V, but the pattern match fails. Thus, in the course of the pattern match, three assignments are made to V: first E, then I, and finally A. The value of V at the end of the attempt to match is A, the last value assigned.

## 4.5 IMMEDIATE ASSIGNMENT AND UNEVALUATED EXPRESSIONS

Unevaluated expressions allow evaluation to be deferred until pattern matching takes place, and immediate value assignment permits the changing of values during pattern matching. Used in conjunction, these two features make possible very powerful types of pattern matching. Suppose, for example, it is necessary to find the string of characters separating any two identical vowels. This rather complicated requirement can be expressed in a simple way by using immediate assignment and unevaluated expressions, as illustrated by the following pattern.

```
        IVWL    =    VOWEL $ V  BREAK(*V) . GAP
```

Suppose the value of TEXT is:

MOUNTAINOUS TERRAIN

The statement

```
        TEXT    IVWL
```

succeeds and assigns UNTAIN to GAP. The process used to arrive at this result is straightforward. VOWEL matches the first O in TEXT. This value is assigned to V. BREAK(*V) is now equivalent to BREAK('O'). This pattern component matches and the cursor is advanced to the second O in TEXT. The pattern match succeeds and the string between the two Os is assigned to GAP.

```
 V  GAP
MOUNTAINOUS TERRAIN
```

## 4.6 PRECEDENCE OF PATTERN-CONSTRUCTING OPERATORS

There are four binary operators used in constructing patterns. They all associate to the left, and have the following relative precedences:

| | |
|---|---|
| $ . | value assignment |
| (blank) | concatenation |
| \| | alternation |

Therefore

```
TVOWEL   =   VOWEL VOWEL . T
```

is equivalent to

```
TVOWEL   =   VOWEL (VOWEL . T)
```

and

```
LINE   =   ':' | BREAK(' ') . L
```

is equivalent to:

```
LINE   =   ':' | (BREAK(' ') . L)
```

Of course, parentheses may be used to group the operands differently.

Ordinarily, arithmetic operators are not used in the same expression with pattern-constructing operators, so the relative precedences of the two types of operators is usually not of concern. However, a table of precedences for all operators is included in Appendix B.

### EXERCISES

4.1. Suppose the value of TEXT is:

```
LET SLEEPING DOGS LIE
```

Follow through the details of pattern matching and the changes in the value of TEXT for successive executions of the following statement:

```
DEL     TEXT     'E'  |  'I'   =                    :S(DEL)
```

**4.2.** Describe briefly what kinds of strings are matched by the following patterns. Assume VOWEL is a pattern as described in Section 4.1.

```
P1   =   VOWEL ARB VOWEL

P2   =   VOWEL LEN(1) ARB VOWEL

P3   =   VOWEL TAB(5) VOWEL

P4   =   TAB(6) VOWEL VOWEL

P5   =   RTAB(3) ARB VOWEL

P6   =   ANY('0123456789')

P7   =   POS(0) P6

P8   =   POS(0) NOTANY('*')

P9   =   SPAN('1234567890') '.'

P10  =   '(' BAL ')'

P11  =   POS(0) '(' BAL ')' RPOS(0)

P12  =   VOWEL $ V BREAK(*V)

P13  =   TAB(9) *DUPL(' ',N)
```

**4.3.** Write patterns that match the following kinds of strings:

(a) Strings that do not end with the character *.
(b) Strings that contain at least two vowels.
(c) Strings longer than 10 characters.
(d) Strings consisting entirely of vowels.
(e) Strings that contain at least three instances of some character.

**4.4.** Write a program to count the number of words on a data file.

**4.5.** Discuss the deficiencies of WPAT as described in Section 4.2.

CHAPTER 5

# Programmer-Defined Functions

Built-in functions provide the means for performing many program operations–trimming and duplicating strings, creating patterns, testing conditions, and so on. There are, of course, many operations for which there are no built-in functions. Each program has different operations to perform, and no matter how many built-in functions are provided, there are always operations that these functions cannot do. Such operations must therefore be programmed using SNOBOL4 statements.

An example is the process of reversing a string end-for-end so that the last character becomes first, and so on. This may be done easily with a few statements. Suppose the string to be reversed is the value of TEXT. A section of program to reverse the value of TEXT is:

```
         REVERSE   =
         STRING    =   TEXT
REVERSE  STRING    LEN(1) . C   =                :F(DONE)
         REVERSE   =   C REVERSE                 :(REVERSE)
DONE     .
         .
         .
```

First the null string is assigned to REVERSE and next a copy of TEXT is assigned to STRING. Characters are taken from STRING one by one and built up in reverse order in

REVERSE. When no characters remain, the process is complete and REVERSE contains the desired reversed copy of TEXT. Note that the value of STRING is destroyed in the process, which is why TEXT itself is not used. Such an operation is easy to program and presents no particular problems. If, however, it is necessary to reverse a string at several different places in the program, then similar statements must be provided in each place, or a way must be found to use a common set of statements. If REVERSE were a built-in function, there would be no problem. Each time it is necessary to reverse a string, a statement such as

```
        RTEXT     =     REVERSE(TEXT)
```

could be used. In fact, SNOBOL4 provides a way of making functions out of sections of SNOBOL4 program so that these sections can be used in exactly this way.

## 5.1 DEFINING FUNCTIONS

A function consisting of a section of a SNOBOL4 program is called a *programmer-defined function.* Several rules must be followed to create such a programmer-defined function. First the built-in function DEFINE must be executed. DEFINE establishes the existence of a programmer-defined function and describes its properties. The argument of DEFINE is a string that looks like a call of the function being defined. For REVERSE, the defining statement might be:

```
        DEFINE('REVERSE(STRING)')
```

REVERSE(STRING) establishes the name of the function, REVERSE, and a name for its argument, STRING. The section of program used to carry out a programmer-defined function is called a *procedure.* There are certain conventions for writing such procedures.

In the first place, the procedure begins with a statement whose label is the same as the name of the function. In the example, this label is REVERSE. When a programmer-defined function is called, execution is suspended at that point and control is transferred to the first statement in the procedure for the function.

Next there must be a way of communicating to the procedure what the values of its arguments are. This is done by using the arguments which are given in the defining statement. In the example above, STRING is the name of the argument. Therefore when REVERSE(TEXT) is called, the value of TEXT is assigned to STRING. This provides a way of *passing the argument* to the procedure, regardless of how REVERSE is called or what string is to be reversed. It is as if the following statement had been executed:

```
        STRING    =     TEXT                          :(REVERSE)
```

Conventions also exist for indicating that the computation in a procedure is complete and that the value computed by the procedure is to be returned to the place of the call. RETURN has a special meaning. A transfer to RETURN does not transfer control to a label

RETURN, but instead signals the completion of the procedure. Whatever value the name of the procedure has at this time is the value returned, and becomes the result of a function call. The statements for reversing a string given earlier can now be modified slightly to follow the rules for a procedure. In fact, they are simpler:

```
REVERSE STRING    LEN(1) . C    =                     :F(RETURN)

        REVERSE    =    C REVERSE                     :(REVERSE)
```

Note that the initial statements given in the earlier program are no longer used. This is possible because certain operations are performed automatically when a programmer-defined function is called. When a statement such as

```
        RTEXT    =    REVERSE(TEXT)
```

is executed, the function call performs the equivalent of the following statements:

```
        SAVE1    =    REVERSE

        REVERSE  =

        SAVE2    =    STRING

        STRING   =    TEXT                            :(REVERSE)
```

These are not real statements, but are only "pseudo-statements" showing what operations are performed. SAVE1 and SAVE2 are not real variables, but only indicate that the values of REVERSE and STRING are saved before transfer to the procedure. Note that the value of REVERSE (the name of the function) is initialized to the null string so that it may be used by the procedure without concern about what its value may have been before the function call.

When the procedure transfers to RETURN, the value of REVERSE supplies the value of the function call. Then the following operations are performed.

```
        STRING   =    SAVE2

        REVERSE  =    SAVE1
```

Execution of the statement

```
        RTEXT    =    REVERSE(TEXT)
```

continues, assigning the reversed string to RTEXT. Note that the values of REVERSE and STRING are saved when the function is called and restored when the function returns. Therefore the function call leaves their values unchanged. Thus the function REVERSE can be used anywhere in the program without fear that it will change the values of REVERSE or STRING. Note, however, that REVERSE uses the name C in the process of its computation. Since the value of C is not saved and restored, the function REVERSE changes C in a *global* sense. The value of C will, in general, be changed by a call of REVERSE. This may be avoided by making C *local* to the procedure in which it is used. This is indicated by appending C to the string which describes the REVERSE function in the defining statement, as follows:

```
        DEFINE('REVERSE(STRING)C')
```

When C is included in this way, its value is saved before transfer to the REVERSE procedure, assigned a null value, and then restored on return from the procedure.

Observe that a programmer-defined function is used in exactly the same way that a built-in function is used. In fact there is no way to tell whether a function is built-in or defined except by looking at the program to see if there is a defining statement and a procedure for it.

Defined functions may have more than one argument; in fact there may be as many arguments as are needed. There may also be many local names. In both cases, the additional names are written in a list, separated by commas. An example is the function MERGE(S1,S2) whose value is a string consisting of alternate characters of S1 and S2. The defining statement is:

```
        DEFINE('MERGE(S1,S2)C1,C2')
```

S1 and S2 are arguments and C1 and C2 are local names. The procedure is:

```
MERGE   S1   LEN(1) . C1   =                       :F(MERND1)

        S2   LEN(1) . C2   =                       :F(MERND2)

        MERGE  =  MERGE C1 C2                      :(MERGE)

MERND1  MERGE  =  MERGE S2                         :(RETURN)

MERND2  MERGE  =  MERGE C1 S1                      :(RETURN)
```

The following calls of MERGE have the values indicated:

```
        MERGE('ABC','012')         A0B1C3

        MERGE('ABC','0')           A0BC

        MERGE('A','012')           A012
```

A defined function may fail in the same way that a built-in predicate fails. Failure is indicated by transferring to FRETURN instead of RETURN. Suppose, in the example above, that MERGE is to return a value only if the lengths of the two arguments are the same, and is to fail otherwise. The procedure could be rewritten as follows:

```
MERGE   EQ(SIZE(S1),SIZE(S2))                    :F(FRETURN)

MERG    S1  LEN(1)  . C1   =                     :F(RETURN)

        S2  LEN(1)  . C2   =

        MERGE  =   MERGE C1 C2                   :(MERG)
```

Now, the value of MERGE('ABC','012') is A0B1C2, but both MERGE('ABC',0) and MERGE('A','012') fail.

Sometimes a function does not need any arguments. Suppose, for example, that a data file contains some records with information to be processed, and other records which are only comments. In this file, comment records begin with a * to distinguish them from information records. A function INFO can be written to read the data file, bypass comment records, and return the next information record. The defining statement and procedure for INFO might be:

```
      DEFINE('INFO()')

              .

              .

              .

INFO    INFO   =    INPUT                        :F(FRETURN)

        INFO   POS(0) '*'                        :S(INFO)F(RETURN)
```

A typical use of INFO is:

```
READ     LINE   =    INFO()                      :F(DONE)
```

Notice that no arguments are specified when INFO is defined or when it is called.

The examples given above deal only with strings, but the arguments of a call to a defined function may be any type of object, and any kind of value may be returned. This is illustrated by the function EITHER(P1,P2) where P1 and P2 are patterns. The function EITHER(P1,P2) returns a pattern that matches either P1 followed by P2 or P2 followed by P1. The defining statement is

```
      DEFINE('EITHER(P1,P2)')
```

and the procedure is:

```
EITHER EITHER   =   (P1 P2)  |  (P2 P1)          :(RETURN)
```

## 5.2 FUNCTIONAL COMPOSITION

One of the reasons for using a function is so that the procedure associated with that function may be called from anywhere in the program. A function call may even occur in another procedure. To see why this may be useful, consider RMERGE(S1,S2) whose value is the same as that of MERGE, except that the result is reversed. It is not a difficult matter to write a procedure to do this, but functions already have been written for merging and reversing strings. Using these functions simplifies the writing of RMERGE. The defining statement is:

```
        DEFINE('MERGE(S1,S2)')
```

The procedure is simply:

```
RMERGE RMERGE  =   REVERSE(MERGE(S1,S2))          :(RETURN)
```

Thus RMERGE calls MERGE to merge S1 and S2 and then calls REVERSE to reverse the result. Note that RMERGE does not need to specify local variables—this is done by MERGE and REVERSE.

This technique of "functional composition" provides a very powerful programming tool, permitting previously defined functions to be used in developing new ones and avoiding repetitious programming.

## 5.3 RECURSIVE FUNCTIONS

If one function can be called while executing another, what prevents a function from calling itself while it is being executed? In fact a function *can* call itself. (This is true in SNOBOL4, but not in all programming languages.) Such a call is a *recursive call*. One could well ask what possible use a recursive call might have. Recursion in functions is, in fact, one of the most powerful of all programming techniques. Recursive definitions are frequently used in mathematics for defining things in terms of themselves. Such definitions are concise and elegant, if apparently circular at first sight. The most familiar recursive definition is that of the *factorial* of a number, written as $n!$ $n!$ is simply the product of all integers from 1 to $n$. That is

$$n! \quad = \quad 1 * 2 * \ldots * n$$

This is not a recursive definition, but uses ellipses (...) to indicate an indefinite repetition. A recursive definition is:

$$0! \quad = \quad 1$$

$$n! \quad = \quad n * (n-1)! \qquad \text{for } n > 0$$

The first line is a special case. The second line defines $n!$ in terms of itself. This definition eventually terminates because the special case $0!$ is reached. For example:

$$4! = 4 * 3! = 4 * 3 * 2! = 4 * 3 * 2 * 1! =$$

$$4 * 3 * 2 * 1 * 0! = 4 * 3 * 2 * 1 * 1 = 24$$

It is actually possible to compute $n!$ by using a function which is based on this recursive definition. The defining statement and procedure are:

```
      DEFINE('F(N)')
        .
        .
        .
F     F  =  EQ(N,0) 1                    :S(RETURN)
      F  =  N * F(N - 1)                 :(RETURN)
```

Following through a case will illustrate how this works. Consider F(4). When F(4) is called, N is assigned the value 4. Since 4 is not equal to zero, the second statement is executed, and is equivalent to:

```
      F  =  4 * F(3)                     :(RETURN)
```

The call F(3) saves the current value of N and then assigns the value 3 to N. Again 3 is not equal to zero and a statement equivalent to

```
      F  =  3 * F(2)                     :(RETURN)
```

is executed. Note that the previous statement has not yet completed, and will not complete until F(3) returns its value. This process continues until F(0) is called. At this point the following statements have been started, but not completed:

```
      F  =  4 * F(3)                     :(RETURN)
      F  =  3 * F(2)                     :(RETURN)
      F  =  2 * F(1)                     :(RETURN)
      F  =  1 * F(0)                     :(RETURN)
```

The call of F(0) stops this "recursive plunge", since the first statement succeeds, and returns the value 1 for F(0). The previous statement then succeeds and returns the value 1 for F(1), and so on. Finally F(3) returns the value 6 and the original call, F(4), returns the desired result, 24.

While this process works as described, and could actually be used to compute *n*! (should one want to), it should be evident that this method is unnecessarily elaborate. A more straightforward procedure is:

```
F       F     =     EQ(N,0) 1                          :S(RETURN)

        F     =     N

F1      N     =     GT(N,1) N - 1                      :F(RETURN)

        F     =     F * N                              :(F1)
```

This type of computation is called *iterative* rather than recursive, since the same operation is performed repeatedly. While this procedure is a trifle longer, it is easier to understand. The iterative technique is also simpler and faster, since the additional function calls in the recursive procedure require the saving and restoring of values.

If iteration has these advantages over recursion, why use recursion at all, then? In simple cases there is usually no reason to use recursion. In complicated problems, however, it may be possible to formulate a recursive solution easily, while an iterative solution may be extremely difficult to formulate. Thus recursion may be a very useful problem-solving tool.

Consider the following example. Arithmetic expressions are usually written in *infix* form with operators between their operands. A simple example is:

```
((V1*V2)-V3)+V4
```

SNOBOL4 uses a similar notation except that blanks are required around the operators. An alternative form places operators in prefix position with operators before their operands. The prefix expression equivalent to the example above is:

```
+(-(*(V1,V2),V3),V4)
```

(Notice that this is essentially a functional notation in which the operators appear where function names ordinarily occur.) Now consider the problem of converting expressions, containing only binary operators, from infix form to prefix form. One operator is simple. For example, `V1*V2` becomes `*(V1,V2)`. Suppose the operators are `+`, `-`, `*`, and `/`. A pattern for matching an operator and its operands is:

```
        INP     =     BAL . L ANY('+-/*') . OP BAL . R
```

The pattern `INP` would not work properly on the example above since the last `BAL` does not match `V4`:

```
      L       R
 _____^_____  ^
((V1*V2)-V3)+V4
```

To be sure the entire string is matched, the pattern may be modified as follows:

```
          INP     =     POS(0) BAL . L ANY('+-/*') . OP BAL . R
+                       RPOS(0)
```

A statement to convert an operator might be:

```
          EXP     INP     =     OP '(' L ',' R ')'
```

The expression above becomes:

```
+(((V1*V2)-V3),V4)
```

The conversion is only partial. The parts of the expression involving * and - have not been converted. The pattern INP cannot be successfully applied again, since the expressions that remain to be transformed are inside parentheses and INP can only match an entire string. What is needed is the conversion of the expressions L and R. Suppose there is a function PRE(EXP) that puts any expression EXP in prefix form. Then the statement above would be:

```
          EXP     INP     =     OP '(' PRE(L) ',' PRE(R) ')'
```

But such a function PRE is exactly what we are writing! The statement above is part of PRE. This is often how recursive procedures are developed; in writing a procedure, the use of the procedure itself is suggested. There is a little more to PRE than is shown above. PRE must be able to handle any expression including one without any operator, and surrounding parentheses in the infix form sometimes get in the way and must be discarded. A defining statement, patterns, and a complete procedure for PRE follow:

```
          DEFINE('PRE(EXP)L,R,OP')

          INP     =     POS(0) BAL . L ANY('+-/*') . OP BAL . R
+                       RPOS(0)

          RPAREN     =     POS(0) '(' BAL . R ')' RPOS(0)
                            .
                            .
                            .
PRE       EXP     RPAREN  =  R
          EXP     INP     =  OP '(' PRE(L) ',' PRE(R) ')'
          PRE     =     EXP                                   :(RETURN)
```

This function does not attempt to determine the precedence and associativity of operators. Hence parentheses must be included in expressions to be transformed. If an expression is surrounded by parentheses, these are removed by the first statement of the function. If the expression contains no operators, it is returned without modification.

## 5.4 PROCEDURES IN PROGRAMS

Procedures for programmer-defined functions are written in SNOBOL4 and are essentially indistinguishable from the rest of the program. The entry labels of functions are identified with the name of the function but are just like any other labels in the program and may be transferred to in the same way as any other labels. In fact all labels in a procedure are "global" in this sense, and are not different from other program labels. Similarly the end of a procedure is not, in general, identifiable. A transfer to RETURN or FRETURN terminates the call of a function, but the end of a procedure is not set off in the program by any special notation. Thus the procedure for a function may be flowed into or transferred to from anywhere in the program. Entering a procedure in this way is usually an accident and results in an error, since the transfer to RETURN or FRETURN cannot be made unless the procedure has been entered by a function call. In fact, an error frequently made by the beginning SNOBOL4 programmer is to place the procedure for a function immediately after the defining statement for the function. A typical example is:

```
         DEFINE('REVERSE(STRING)C')

REVERSE STRING    LEN(1) . C    =                        :F(RETURN)

         REVERSE    =    C REVERSE                        :(REVERSE)
```

In this case, after executing the DEFINE function, execution continues with the statement labeled REVERSE. If the value of STRING is null, as is likely to be the case, an attempt to transfer to RETURN is made, which is an error since the procedure for REVERSE has been flowed into, not entered by a call. Thus, the procedures for functions should not be in the main line of flow of the program. Where to put the procedures is a matter of taste. Some programmers prefer to put all procedures near the end of the program where they will not be executed accidentally. Other programmers prefer to keep the procedures with their defining statements. Since the defining statements must be executed (usually early in program execution) and the procedures themselves should not be executed until they are called, gotos may be provided to branch around the procedures. A typical example is:

```
         DEFINE('REVERSE(STRING)C')                          :(REVEND)

REVERSE  STRING   LEN(1) . C   =                             :F(RETURN)

         REVERSE   =   C REVERSE                             :(REVERSE)

REVEND   .

         .

         .
```

After DEFINE is executed, control is transferred to REVEND, bypassing the procedure itself.

It is also worth remembering that all program labels must be different. Labels in procedures are not different from labels elsewhere in a program. Consequently two procedures may share a common section of program and both may branch to the same location. Since all labels are global, there is no way to provide a local label for a procedure in the same sense that a variable may be made local.

## EXERCISES

**5.1.** Write a function MATRIX(C,N,M) that prints an N by M matrix of the character which is the value of C. See Exercise 3.3.

**5.2.** Write a function DELETE(S,C) whose value is the result of deleting all occurrences of the character which is the value of C from the string which is the value of S.

**5.3.** Write a function SUBSTR(S,N,M) whose value is the substring of S which begins at the Nth character of S and is M characters long.

**5.4.** Write a predicate PALIN(S) that succeeds if S is a palindrome and fails otherwise. See Exercise 2.4.

**5.5.** Sometimes blanks are ignored in determining if a string is a palindrome. Thus

```
WAS IT A RAT I SAW
```

could be considered a palindrome. Modify the solution of Exercise 5.4 to test for this type of palindrome.

**5.6.** The *Fibonacci Numbers* are defined as follows:

$$f(0) = 0$$

$$f(1) = 1$$

$$f(n+1) = f(n)+f(n-1) \quad n \geq 1$$

Write a function F(N) whose value is the Nth Fibonacci Number. Compute F(6).

5.7. Postfix form is similar to prefix form, except that operators are written after their operands instead of before them. For example, the infix expression

```
((V1*V2)-V3)+V4
```

has the postfix equivalent:

```
(((V1,V2)*,V3)-,V4)+
```

Write a function POST(EXP) that converts expressions in *prefix* form to postfix form.

CHAPTER 6

# Arrays, Tables, and Defined Data Objects

So far, the only variables used in this book have been names and, for special purposes, keywords. A variable provides a way of keeping track of a value and of referring to that value when it is needed. In most cases, names serve this purpose well. In some instances, however, several values are logically related to each other and it is useful to have a single object associated with all of them. SNOBOL4 provides three ways for referring to such collections of values: arrays, tables, and programmer-defined data objects.

## 6.1 ARRAYS

An array is a collection of values identified by a single name. Individual values are referenced by means of a *subscript* applied to that name. The values in an array can be thought of as being arranged in order by the integers 1, 2, 3, and so on. If RANK is the name of an array, the individual values in RANK are indicated by RANK<1>, RANK<2>, RANK<3>, and so on. The "angular brackets" enclose integer subscripts which identify the particular values. The term subscript is used because of the relation to the mathematical subscript notation in which values would be designated as $\text{RANK}_1$, $\text{RANK}_2$, $\text{RANK}_3$, and so on. Since there is no convenient way of representing a subscript directly on a computer, the angular brackets are used instead. The meaning is the same.

An array is associated with a name by executing a statement such as:

```
      RANK      =     ARRAY('10')
```

ARRAY is a built-in function that creates an array. The value of the argument of ARRAY is a string that determines how many values the array has. The statement above creates an array of 10 values. The assignment associates this array with the name RANK.

Subsequently, the values of RANK are referred to as RANK<1>, RANK<2>, . . . , RANK<10>. Such constructions are called *array references*. When an array is created, all values are null. Values may be changed by assignment statements. An example is

```
          RANK<3>     =    'SERGEANT'
```

which makes SERGEANT the third value in RANK. This statement illustrates that each value in RANK has an associated variable. RANK<3>, for example, is one of these.

Since there are only ten variables in RANK, what happens if an array reference such as RANK<12> is attempted? Such an array reference fails. In general, if the subscript is too large or too small (zero, for example) the array reference fails. Such a subscript is said to be *out of bounds* for that array. Failure of an array reference, like other failures, can be used to select a conditional goto. This failure is particularly useful in referencing an array iteratively. Suppose SQUARE is an array of 20 values which is to contain the squares of the first 20 integers. The following statements could be used to assign these values.

```
          I      =     1

PUTSQ     SQUARE<I>     =     I * I                      :F(DONE)

          I   = I     I + 1                              :(PUTSQ)

DONE        .

            .

            .
```

The statement PUTSQ assigns the square of the subscript I to each array value, and I is incremented in a loop. When I reaches 21, however, the attempt to reference the twenty-first value fails and the loop is broken. Notice that it is not necessary to know how large SQUARE is. The loop above works for an array of any size, which can be very useful.

Although ordinarily when an array is created all values are null, another initial value may be provided. This initial value is specified in the second argument of the ARRAY function. For example

```
          SUMS    =    ARRAY('100',0)
```

creates an array of one hundred values, all of which are zero. Note that the null value, in case the second argument is omitted, follows naturally from the convention that an omitted trailing argument is assumed to be null.

Counting the words of each length that appear in text is another example of the use of arrays. The pattern WPAT given in Section 4.2 can be applied to data read from the input file. A simple program is:

```
         LETTER    =    'ABCDEFGHIJKLMNOPQRSTUVWXYZ'
         WPAT   =   BREAK(LETTER)  SPAN(LETTER) . WORD
         LENGTH  =    ARRAY('10',0)
READ     TEXT   =   INPUT                               :F(PRINT)
         OUTPUT  =    TEXT
NEXTW    TEXT   WPAT   =                                :F(READ)
         N   =   SIZE(WORD)
         LENGTH<N>   =   LENGTH<N> + 1                  :(NEXTW)
PRINT    I   =   1
         OUTPUT   =
         OUTPUT   =   'LENGTH    COUNT'
PRINTW   OUTPUT   =   '   ' I '          ' LENGTH<1>    :F(END)
         I   =   I + 1                                  :(PRINTW)
END
```

A typical output from this program follows:

```
THERE WAS AN OLD MAN OF NANTUCKET
WHO KEPT ALL HIS CASH IN A BUCKET;
  BUT HIS DAUGHTER, NAMED NAN,
  RAN AWAY WITH A MAN --
AND AS FOR THE BUCKET, NANTUCKET.
```

```
LENGTH     COUNT

  1          2

  2          5

  3          14

  4          4

  5          2

  6          1

  7          1

  8          1

  9          2

  10         0
```

Note that the failure of an array reference which is out of bounds is used to terminate the printing loop.

The subscript of an array reference need not be given explicitly as illustrated in the program above, but may be the value of an expression computed in the reference itself. Thus the two statements

```
        N     =     SIZE(WORD)

        LENGTH<N>     =     LENGTH<N> + 1
```

could be combined in one statement:

```
        LENGTH<SIZE(N)>    =    LENGTH<SIZE(N)> + 1
```

Note, however, that if this is done, SIZE(N) must be computed twice.

The arrays described above are referred to as *linear* arrays, since the subscripts can be laid out on a line, in a one-dimensional fashion, as illustrated in Figure 6.1.

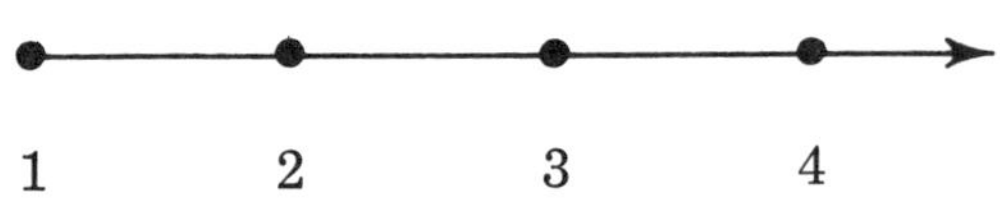


**Figure 6.1** Subscripts of a Linear Array

This geometrical concept obviously can be generalized to two dimensions, as illustrated in Figure 6.2, in which pairs of integers correspond to positions in space.

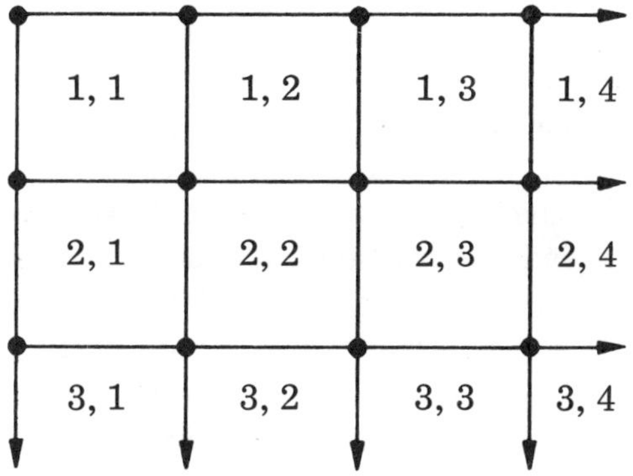


**Figure 6.2** Subscripts of a Two-Dimensional Array

SNOBOL4 provides for two-dimensional arrays in which two subscripts are used, one for each dimension. Such an array is assigned to a name by a statement such as the following:

```
RECTANGLE   =   ARRAY('3,4')
```

The value of the argument of the function ARRAY, in this case, is a string consisting of two numbers, separated by commas. These numbers determine the size of the array in each of its two dimensions. RECTANGLE becomes the name of a 3-by-4 array. Array references that are in bounds are RECTANGLE<1,1>, . . . , RECTANGLE<3,4>. Thus the "last" value in this array corresponds to the integers which are given in the argument of the ARRAY function. Two-dimensional arrays are useful for representing values that are naturally thought of as laid out in two dimensions. A typical case is a checkerboard, which can be thought of as an 8-by-8 array of squares.

Note that the two dimensions are specified in the first argument. The comma is in a data string, and hence there is only one argument in the call of ARRAY above. On the other hand

```
X   =   ARRAY('3',4)
```

creates a linear array of three elements, each of which has the initial value 4.

The extension of arrays from one to two dimensions can be generalized to any number of dimensions: three, four, and so on. The argument of ARRAY simply lists the extent of each dimension, with separating commas. References to such arrays require correspondingly more subscripts.

## 6.2 TABLES

The values in an array may be considered as being arranged in a neat geometrical order. Integer subscripts are associated with the positions of these values accordingly. In some cases, however, there are collections of data that have no natural geometric interpretation and in which integer subscripts are not appropriate. Consider the problem of analyzing text and counting the number of times each word occurs. For example, SOME might occur twice, PEOPLE three times, and so on. The desired results are counts, which form a natural collection of values. Ideally these values might be related to a single name, COUNT, with appropriate subscripts. The subscripts, however, should be the words SOME, PEOPLE, and so on, not integers. For this purpose, a *table* may be used. A table is similar to a linear array, except that the subscripts need not be integers. A table is assigned to a name by a statement such as:

```
        CØUNT     =    TABLE()
```

TABLE is a built-in function that creates a table. TABLE requires no argument, since a table has no fixed size; it grows as necessary. Values in a table are referenced in the same way that values in a linear array are referenced, except that the subscripts need not be integers. For example the statement

```
        COUNT<'SOME'>     =    COUNT<'SOME'> + 1
```

increments the "SOMEth" value in COUNT.

As mentioned above, tables have no fixed size. A value for a subscript is created simply by using that subscript. Such a value is initially null, but it may be changed by an assignment statement as illustrated above. The capability of a table to expand as necessary is very useful when dealing with a problem such as word counting, where the words that may appear cannot be determined in advance. Different texts have different words. There are so many words that might occur that it is useless to try to list all of them explicitly in a program.

A program for counting the number of times each word occurs in text is easily obtained by minor modification to the word-length program given in the last section. Using a table, COUNT, instead of an array, LENGTH, the statement to increment the count for a word becomes:

```
        COUNT<WORD>     =    COUNT<WORD> + 1
```

The statement increments the count for the word, whatever the value of WORD is. When a word is used for the first time, its initial value automatically becomes the null string. Since the null string is numerically equal to zero, the count for the word becomes one. Thus, using WPAT given in Section 6.1, counting words can be done by the following statements:

```
                •
                •
                •
        COUNT    =   TABLE()
READ    TEXT   =   INPUT                                :F(PRINT)
        OUTPUT   =   TEXT
NEXTW   TEXT   WPAT   =                                 :F(READ)
        COUNT<WORD>   =   COUNT<WORD> + 1               :(NEXTW)
PRINT           •
                •
                •
```

The fact that simply using a subscript in a table reference creates a value for that subscript produces an interesting problem. When word counting is complete, certain words have been used as subscripts for the table. How can the words that have been used as subscripts be determined? Consider some hypothetical subscripts and their corresponding values as shown in Figure 6.3.

```
YOU      2
CAN      1
FOOL     2
SOME     2
OF       5
THE      6
PEOPLE   3
ALL      4
TIME     3
AND      1
BUT      1
CANNOT   1
```

**Figure 6.3** Subscripts and Values in a Table

This arrangement can be thought of as two columns of eight rows each, suggesting a geometrical interpretation as a two-dimensional, 12-by-2, array.

SNOBOL4 provides a way of creating just such an array from a table. The built-in function CONVERT is used as is illustrated by the following statement:

```
          RESULT   =   CONVERT(COUNT,'ARRAY')
```

The first argument of CONVERT is the table to be converted. The second argument is a string that indicates that the result is to be an array. The value returned by CONVERT is an n-by-2 array if there are n subscripts with values in the table. Subscripts which have null values are omitted in the conversion process. If there are no subscripts with nonnull values, CONVERT fails. If the values in COUNT are those given in Figure 6.3, the value assigned to RESULT in the statement above is a 12-by-2 array. The value of RESULT<1,1> is YOU, the value of RESULT<1,2> is 2, the value of RESULT<2,1> is CAN, and so on. In general, the first subscript of the array corresponds to subscripts in the table, and the second subscript of the array corresponds to values in the table. A complete program for counting words and printing the results follows.

```
        LETTER   =   'ABCDEFGHIJKLMNOPQRSTUVWXYZ'
        WPAT   =   BREAK(LETTER)  SPAN(LETTER) . WORD
        COUNT   =   TABLE()
READ    TEXT   =   INPUT                                :F(PRINT)
        OUTPUT   =   TEXT
NEXTW   TEXT   WPAT   =                                 :F(READ)
        COUNT WORD   =   COUNT<WORD> + 1                :(NEXTW)
PRINT   RESULT   =   CONVERT(COUNT,'ARRAY')             :F(NONE)
        OUTPUT   =
        OUTPUT   =   'WORD COUNT'
        OUTPUT   =
        I   =   1
PRINTC  OUTPUT   =   RESULT<I,1>  '-'  RESULT<I,2>      :F(END)
        I   =   I + 1                                   :(PRINTC)
NONE    OUTPUT   =   'THERE ARE NO WORDS'
END
```

Typical printed output is:

```
YOU CAN FOOL SOME OF THE PEOPLE ALL OF THE TIME,

AND ALL OF THE PEOPLE SOME OF THE TIME; BUT

YOU CANNOT FOOL ALL OF THE PEOPLE ALL THE TIME.

WORD COUNT

YOU-2

CAN-1

FOOL-2

SOME-2

OF-5

THE-6

PEOPLE-3

ALL-4

TIME-3

AND-1

BUT-1

CANNOT-1
```

## 6.3 PROGRAMMER-DEFINED DATA OBJECTS

Frequently members of a group of data objects have a number of attributes in common. For example, language analysis might involve study of the sentences in a text, where each sentence might have certain attributes of interest. Such properties might be the type of sentence (declarative, imperative, and so forth), the length (number of words), the subject, predicate, and object.

Consider a specific sentence:

QUOTES ENCLOSE THE VALUE

The attributes could be assigned to names chosen for their mnemonic values:

```
TYPE    =   'DECL'

LENGTH   =   4

SUBJ    =   'QUOTES'

PRED    =   'ENCLOSE'

OBJ    =   'THE VALUE'
```

DECL is an abbreviation for "declarative".

Different sentences would have different values for these attributes. Analysis of a text might involve determining the attributes for each sentence and then comparing the results. For example, the number of sentences of each type might be of interest, as well as the average sentence length, and so forth. The problem is that each sentence has attributes TYPE, LENGTH, and so forth, while the names TYPE, LENGTH, and so forth can only have one value at a time.

SNOBOL4 provides *programmer-defined data types* for situations in which several objects all have the same attributes. A programmer-defined data type is essentially a collection of attributes, called *fields*, which allow a variety of values to be associated with one object in the manner suggested above. A programmer-defined type is created by executing the built-in function DATA which defines the data type in much the same way that DEFINE defines a function. Each defined data type has a name and fields. For the example above, a natural choice for the name of the data type would be SENTENCE. Using obvious abbreviations, the fields might be TYPE, LENGTH, SUBJ, PRED, OBJ. The DATA function has an argument which is a string consisting of the name followed by the fields enclosed in parentheses. For the example above, the data-defining statement might be:

```
DATA('SENTENCE(TYPE,LENGTH,SUBJ,PRED,OBJ)')
```

The fields can be arranged in any order, but the order must be remembered. It is often convenient to put frequently used fields first.

The DATA function performs several tasks so that the new data type can be used. First, DATA defines an *object-creation* function whose name is the same as the name of the data type. This object-creation function is used to create objects of the new type. The arguments of the object-creation function assign values to the fields corresponding to the argument of DATA. Thus

```
S  =  SENTENCE('DECL',4,'QUOTES','ENCLOSE','THE VALUE')
```

creates a SENTENCE and assigns it to S. The value of the first field, TYPE, is DECL, and so on.

DATA also defines *field functions* that can be used to refer to the fields of an object. For example

```
OUTPUT    =    SUBJ(S)
```

prints QUOTES.

Assignments can be made to the fields of a defined object also. For example

```
PRED(S)    =    'DELIMIT'
```

changes the PRED field of S so that S corresponds to the sentence:

QUOTES DELIMIT THE VALUE

Since values can be assigned to fields in this way, fields are variables in the same sense that names, keywords, array references, and table references are variables.

If a field is omitted when an object-creation function is called, that field is assigned a null value automatically. As an extreme case,

```
T    =    SENTENCE()
```

creates a SENTENCE in which all fields are null. Values for these fields can subsequently be assigned as, for example, by the statements:

```
TYPE(T)    =    'IMP'

LENGTH(T)    =    2

PRED(T)    =    'ECCE'

OBJ(T)    =    'HOMO'
```

The corresponding sentence is ECCE HOMO, which is imperative and has no explicit subject. Since no value is assigned to the SUBJ, that field is null. The same SENTENCE could be created by the statement:

```
T    =    SENTENCE('IMP',2,,'ECCE','HOMO')
```

Notice that the third field, SUBJ, is left null.

### Structures

The values of the fields in the preceding example were strings and integers. Fields may also refer to other defined objects. This leads to the idea of one object "pointing to" another and permits the representation of complex structures using defined objects. The following example illustrates this use of defined objects.

Consider a structure called a *binary tree.* Such a structure consists of *nodes* connected together according to certain rules. A node may have two *sons,* a *left son* and a *right son.* Figure 6.4 illustrates a node A, its left son B, and its right son C. A is the *father* of B and C. The relationships among the nodes are indicated by the position of the nodes and the connecting lines.

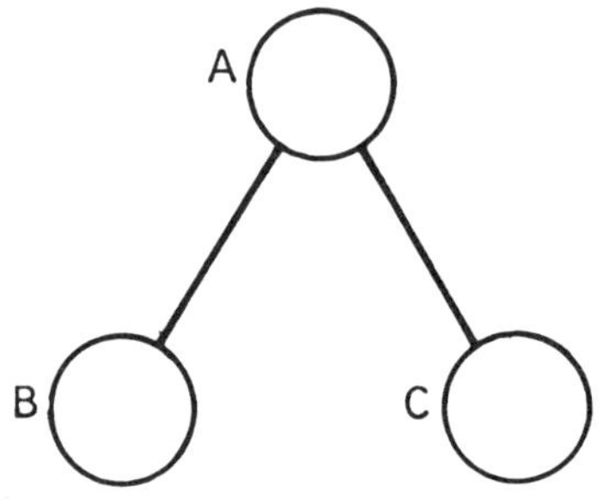


**Figure 6.4** A Node and its Sons

Since B and C are nodes, they may have sons also, and so on. A typical binary tree is illustrated in Figure 6.5.

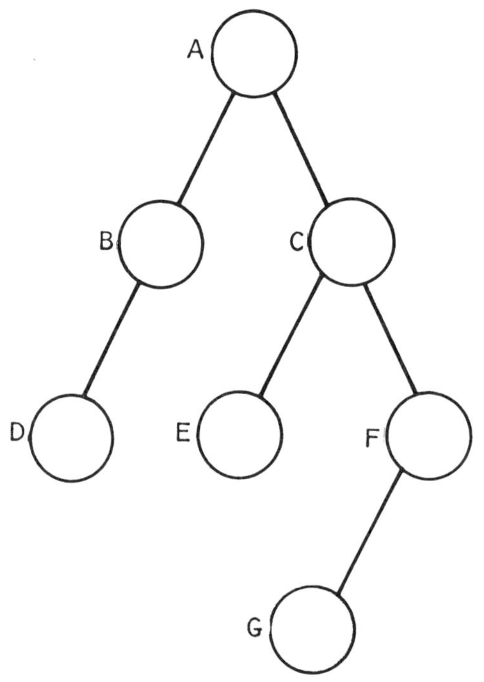


**Figure 6.5** A Binary Tree

Notice that a node need not have both types of sons. Nodes that have no sons are called *leaves.* A node that has no father is called a *root.* (This terminology, while fairly standard in the field, is a polyglot taken from the notation for botanical and genealogical trees. Binary trees are customarily drawn as shown with their roots at the top.) In Figure 6.5, A is a root and D, E, and G are leaves.

For computational purposes, a tree is a structure that can be used to represent the relationship between data items. To incorporate the data items, each node may be thought of as having a value which is depicted within the circle representing the node. One use of such a tree is to represent arithmetic expressions containing binary operators. The expression

```
(X*3)-((Y/2)+(4*Z))
```

can be represented by a binary tree as shown in Figure 6.6.

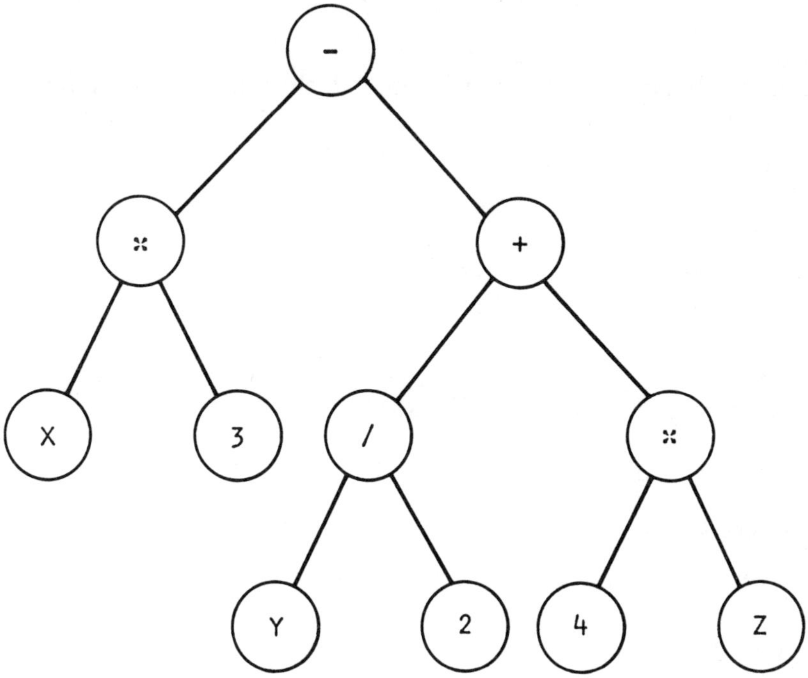


**Figure 6.6** A Tree of Values

Such a structure can easily be represented by using programmer-defined data objects.

The basic data object in a tree is the node. These nodes have certain attributes. In general a node may have a left son, a right son, a father, and a value. Therefore the following statement could be used for describing nodes:

```
DATA('NODE(VALUE,LSON,RSON,FATHER)')
```

The fields LSON, RSON, and FATHER given here are quite different, at least conceptually, from the fields for the data type SENTENCE. There the values of fields were all familiar objects: strings or integers. Here, as illustrated in Figure 6.7, the left son of a node is a node, illustrated by an arrow pointing from one node to another. Such relationships are easily established among NODEs, although it requires a little faith at first.

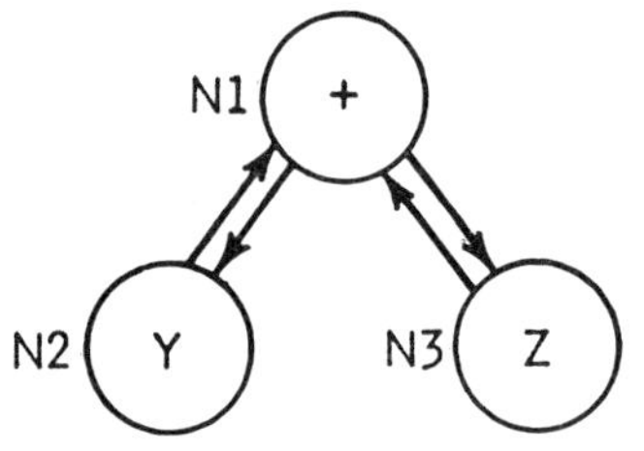


**Figure 6.7** Pointers in a Binary Tree

To construct the binary tree given in Figure 6.7, the relationships implied in that diagram must be established. First we create three nodes with the values indicated.

```
N1  =  NODE('+')
N2  =  NODE('Y')
N3  =  NODE('Z')
```

Now to connect these together, the fields must be set up.

```
LSON(N1)    =   N2
RSON(N1)    =   N3
FATHER(N2)  =   N1
FATHER(N3)  =   N1
```

These fields reference, or point to, other nodes. For example the FATHER of N3 points to node N1.

The tree could be obtained somewhat more simply by supplying some of the field values when the NODEs are created. One way to do this is:

```
N1  =  NODE('+')
N2  =  NODE('Y',,,N1)
N3  =  NODE('Z',,,N1)
LSON(N1)   =  N2
RSON(N1)   =  N3
```

Once N1 has been created, it can be supplied as the FATHER field when creating N2 and N3. Alternatively, the nodes could be created in a different order:

```
N2    =    NODE('Y')

N3    =    NODE('Z')

N1    =    NODE('+',N2,N3)

FATHER(N2)    =    N1

FATHER(N3)    =    N1
```

In any event, a node cannot be given in a field until it has been created, so some of the fields have to be filled in after the nodes are created.

If no value is assigned to a field, it has a null value as was mentioned earlier. Since not every node has a left son, right son, and father, it is convenient to indicate a missing relationship by a null value of the field. There is no reason why a missing relationship has to be represented by a null value, but it is a common convention.

There are no built-in functions for performing operations on specific programmer-defined data objects. Such objects may have many meanings and uses which constitute extensions to SNOBOL4. It is therefore natural to provide programmer-defined functions to perform operations that may be needed for specific objects. In the case of binary trees, for example, it might be necessary to determine if a node is a leaf. The following predicate could be used for this purpose.

```
         DEFINE('LEAF(NODE)')
                  .
                  .
                  .
LEAF     (IDENT(LSON(NODE)) IDENT(RSON(NODE)))
+                                                   :S(RETURN)F(FRETURN)
```

Similarly, a function to add a pair of nodes as sons to a leaf node might be:

```
        DEFINE('ADSONS(N1,N2,N3)')

                  .

                  .

                  .

ADSONS  LSON(N1)    =    N2

        RSON(N1)    =    N3

        FATHER(N2)  =     N1

        FATHER(N3)  =     N1                        :(RETURN)
```

The functions to be written depend, of course, on the nature of the data objects and the operations to be performed.

The examples of the data objects SENTENCE and NODE illustrate only two possible uses of programmer-defined objects. There is an endless variety of similar uses, depending on the data to be represented and manipulated.

## EXERCISES

**6.1.** In the program that uses an array to keep a count of word lengths, what happens if a word more than ten characters long is encountered? What might be done in such a case?

**6.2.** Set up an array whose values are the first five powers of the integers from 1 to 10.

**6.3.** Write a program to count characters on a data file. Print the counts.

**6.4.** Write a program to count the number of occurrences of each four-letter word on a data file.

**6.5.** A *complex number* consists of two parts: a real number and an imaginary number. Complex numbers are usually written in the form $a + bi$ where $a$ is the real part and $b$ is the imaginary part. Create a representation for complex numbers so that they can be manipulated in a program.

**6.6.** Write functions ADD, SUB, MPY, and DIV for adding, subtracting, multiplying, and dividing complex numbers. If necessary, refer to an elementary mathematics text for definitions of these operations.

**6.7.** Write a predicate IDSUBJ(S1,S2) that succeeds if the subjects of SENTENCEs S1 and S2 are identical, and fails otherwise.

**6.8.** Write a function XSONS(NODE) that exchanges the left and right sons of a node in a binary tree.

CHAPTER 7

# Input and Output

Input and output may be performed easily by appropriate use of the three names INPUT, OUTPUT, and PUNCH. Files are read, written, and punched, record-by-record, each time one of these names is used. For most programs these three names are adequate. There is really nothing sacred about these names, however: input, output, and punch files are common to almost all computer installations and the names INPUT, OUTPUT, and PUNCH were chosen for their mnemonic value.

## 7.1 INPUT AND OUTPUT ASSOCIATIONS

The association of a name with a file makes input or output possible, and the names INPUT, OUTPUT, and PUNCH are associated automatically with their corresponding files. Other names can be associated with files, however. This is done by executing a built-in function that creates the type of association desired. Basically there are just two types of associations: input and output. (OUTPUT and PUNCH are just two varieties of output.) Correspondingly there are two association functions, INPUT and OUTPUT (not to be confused with the I/O-associated names INPUT and OUTPUT). Any name can be given an input association by executing the built-in function INPUT. An example is:

```
INPUT('CARD')
```

After executing this statement, CARD is input-associated and every reference to CARD reads an input record in the same way as reference to the name INPUT. Thus

```
LINE    =    CARD                                  :F(DONE)
```

reads a record and assigns it to LINE. The input association for CARD does not interfere with the input association for INPUT. Either or both can be used for reading input, and both can be read from the same file. Many names can, in fact, be associated with the same file. For example, the statements

```
INPUT('CARD1')

INPUT('CARD2')

INPUT('CARD3')
```

associate the three names CARD1, CARD2, and CARD3 with the input file.

Just as several names can be associated with the input file, so can several names be associated with the output file. Use of the built-in function OUTPUT is illustrated by:

```
OUTPUT('LINE')
```

Subsequently, the statement

```
LINE   =   CARD                                              :F(DONE)
```

reads a line and prints it.

## 7.2 FILE NUMBERS

For most programs it is sufficient to know that there are input, output, and punch files. Some installations require control cards that specify these files, but such requirements vary from location to location and are not part of the SNOBOL4 language.

Some programs, however, need to use other files. Data to be processed may be on a magnetic tape, for example. Similarly, the results of running a program may have to be saved on a tape or disk. For such cases, more must be known about files and how the running SNOBOL4 program communicates with its environment. Ways of talking about files vary from language to language and from installation to installation. SNOBOL4 uses an old-fashioned, but simple, scheme which is the same as the one used by the FORTRAN programming language. Files are identified by integers. The integer to be used for identifying a particular file varies from installation to installation and can usually be changed by control cards. Most commonly, the identifying integers are:

| *File* | *Integer* |
|---|---|
| input | 5 |
| printed output | 6 |
| punched output | 7 |

The identifying integers are used in the second argument of the INPUT and OUTPUT functions. Thus

```
OUTPUT('RECORD',7)
```

associates the name RECORD with the punch output file. If no second argument is provided, it is assumed to be 5 for INPUT and 6 for OUTPUT. This convention, which simplifies associations for the commonest cases, was used in the preceding section.

The major advantage of file numbers is that they provide the capability of referring to files other than the standard ones. For example if a tape is to be read, it might be identified by the integer 10. Then the association

```
INPUT('DATA',10)
```

associates the name DATA with the tape so that every time the name DATA is used, a record is read from the tape. Similarly

```
OUTPUT('RESULT',20)
```

might be used to associate the name RESULT with a tape to be created, identified by the number 20.

These associations connect SNOBOL4 names with files identified by the given numbers. It is another problem to connect these numbers with the actual files (such as tapes). The way in which this connection is done depends on the particular computer installation and varies considerably.

## 7.3 RECORD LENGTHS, CARRIAGE CONTROL, AND FORMATS

### Record Lengths

For the standard files, input and punch records are usually 80 characters long, corresponding to the standard punched card. The length of printed records is usually longer and varies from installation to installation. A typical length is 133. The standard lengths are provided automatically. When a record is read in, it is 80 characters long. When a string is punched out, blanks are added as necessary to make up 80 characters. If the string is longer than 80 characters, it is put out in 80-character sections. Thus, punching a very long string may produce several records. Similarly, if a string to be printed is longer than the record length specified for printing, the string is divided into sections of the specified length and printed on successive lines. Printed output is somewhat more complicated because of the properties of printers, the physical devices which do the printing.

### Carriage Control

Most printers print a line at a time rather than a character at a time like a typewriter. Printers also have the capability of skipping a line or more, or even skipping to the top of a new page (called "page ejection"). These capabilities are quite important in creating printed output in the desired format. In order to determine whether to single space, double space, or eject to the top of a new page, the printer must be given control information. By a standard convention, used at almost every installation, the first character of every print line is used for this purpose. This first character is the carriage control character and instead of being printed, it is used to control the printer. Certain characters have standard meanings. The common ones are:

| | |
|---|---|
| blank | single space |
| 0 | double space |
| 1 | eject to new page |

While carriage control makes it possible to print lines on a page in the desired way, it is often a great bother. Since the first character of every print line is consumed for carriage control, a special character has to be put in front of each line before it can be printed. For values assigned to OUTPUT, a blank is appended automatically by SNOBOL4, giving single spacing. The programmer who is satisfied with single-spaced output may be spared the next topic: formats.

### Formats

A format is a specification describing how a string is to be output. The formats used by SNOBOL4 are based on those used by FORTRAN. Since SNOBOL4 output is simple, a programmer need not be an expert on formats. In fact, only a small class of FORTRAN formats can be used in SNOBOL4. The description that follows is intentionally superficial. The programmer interested in formats should study appropriate FORTRAN manuals.

One of the main purposes of formats in SNOBOL4 is to specify the length of output records. The simplest form of a format is (*n*A1) where *n* is an integer specifying how long an output record is to be. For example (72A1) specifies a record of 72 characters. The enclosing parentheses are required. The A1 merely specifies that the string is to be considered as single "alphanumeric" characters (as opposed to just numbers, for example). While FORTRAN permits other specifications, (*n*A1) should be used in all formats used in SNOBOL4 except where other formats are expressly permitted by a particular installation.

Ordinarily, formats are not required. Where departures from standard output are necessary, a format is given as the third argument of OUTPUT when an output association is made. For example, the statement

```
OUTPUT('PUNCH',7,'(72A1)')
```

changes the length of punched output records from 80 to 72.

Similarly

```
OUTPUT('TAPE',30,'(100A1)')
```

associates TAPE with an output file identified by the number 30 and specifies that output records are to be 100 characters long.

Carriage control can be explicitly specified in a format. An example is the format (1H0,132A1). The second part of the format specifies a length as before. The first part, 1H0, is a way of specifying the carriage control character 0. The 1H means that one character following the H is taken to be a ("Hollerith") literal, namely a zero. This rather curious notation belongs to FORTRAN and is equivalent to the SNOBOL4 notation '0'. The entire format specifies that an output line is to begin with a zero and have 132 characters of the output string appended to it. The 0 for (double-spaced) carriage control is then provided automatically when output is performed. For example

```
OUTPUT('DOUBLE',6,'(1H0,132A1)')
```

associates DOUBLE with the standard print output file. Executing the statement

```
DOUBLE    =    'RESULTS'
```

outputs the string 0RESULTS. The first character provides control to the printer, and causes a line to be skipped before printing RESULTS.

A useful output association is

```
OUTPUT('TITLE',6,'(1H1,132A1)')
```

which provides the carriage control character 1 each time TITLE is assigned a value. The 1 causes the value of TITLE to be printed at the top of a new page.

The string appended at the beginning of a format need not be a single character, but may be any data string. The integer before the H indicates the number of characters following that are to be taken literally. An example is:

```
OUTPUT('ANSWER',6,'(7H TOTAL=,126A1)')
```

This association provides for appending seven characters on output to every value assigned to ANSWER. The first character is carriage control for single spacing and the next six characters provide identifying information. The statement

```
ANSWER    =    7
```

prints:

```
TOTAL=7
```

Formats may appear to be mysterious, and, since they were borrowed from FORTRAN, are alien to the SNOBOL4 language. Most formatting problems can be handled by blindly following the rules given above without understanding the underlying reasons. FORTRAN manuals should be consulted for a more thorough understanding of formats.

Nonstandard input record lengths may be specified also, but formats are not necessary —an integer for the third argument of INPUT is used instead. For example

```
INPUT('INPUT',5,72)
```

specifies that only 72 characters are to be read on input. If the input file has longer records, the remaining characters are discarded.

## 7.4 DETACHING NAMES AND REPOSITIONING FILES

Sometimes it is useful to be able to remove an input or output association. This is done by the built-in function DETACH. For example

```
DETACH('OUTPUT')
```

removes the output association for OUTPUT. After executing this statement, values assigned to OUTPUT do not produce printed output. Any associated name, whether the association is for input or output, may be detached. Associations may be reestablished by subsequently executing an appropriate association function.

As records on a file are read, the position in the file advances. Eventually the end of the data may be reached, indicated by failure when input is attempted. If a file is being written, records are appended to the file. Sometimes it is useful to go back to the beginning of a file and read it again, or read a file that has been written. The process of repositioning the file at the beginning is called rewinding and is performed by the built-in function REWIND. The argument of REWIND is the number of the file to be rewound. For example

```
REWIND(10)
```

rewinds the file numbered 10.

It is a good practice to detach any names that have been used to write a file before rewinding that file for reading. Thus, if RESULT is output associated with file number 20, and it is desired to rewind and read file 20, the following statements might be used.

```
DETACH('RESULT')

REWIND(20)

INPUT('REREAD',20,80)
```

Subsequently, REREAD may be used to read records written on file 20 by RESULT.

## 7.5 OUTPUT OF VARIOUS TYPES OF DATA

Anything that is output must be in the form of a string; that is the nature of the output process. Thus output of strings is natural and is governed by formats described in the preceding section. If any other type of value is assigned to an output-associated name, that data type is converted to a string which is then output. For example

```
        OUTPUT    =    1000
```

prints:

```
1000
```

In general, integers and real numbers are converted to strings for output in the same way that they are converted to strings if they are used in an operation such as concatenation.

In the case of other types of data, there is no natural representation of values as strings. For example, a pattern or a programmer-defined data type has no really meaningful string representation. In case such a value is assigned to an output-associated name, the string put out is the data type of the object. For example,

```
        OUTPUT    =    LEN(3)
```

prints:

```
PATTERN
```

In the case of an array, the array prototype is printed also. For example, if A is a linear array of 100 values,

```
        OUTPUT    =   A
```

prints:

```
ARRAY('100')
```

In particular, note that the array values are not printed automatically. To print the values in an array, each value must be assigned to OUTPUT separately.

### EXERCISES

7.1. Write a program to copy a data file of 200-character records from file number 10 to file number 20.

7.2. Write a program to read a data file and print it one character per line.

**7.3.** Write a statement that associates ATTENTION with the print file and provides for five stars in front of every value assigned to ATTENTION.

**7.4.** Write a function ARYPRT(A) that prints the values of the array A. Assume A is linear.

CHAPTER 8

# Programming Techniques

Computer programming is both a challenging and rewarding occupation. Many programming problems, such as those given in this book, are small. Other problems are much more complicated and require large programs for their solution. Programming techniques become of paramount importance in really large programs. Small problems often can be solved in almost any fashion, but large problems often cannot be solved satisfactorily unless good techniques are used. Proficiency in programming is largely a matter of experience, but there are some principles that are important.

Techniques that can be used in programming to achieve the best results are somewhat dependent on the nature of the problem to be solved and on the programming language that is used. This chapter is mainly concerned with programming techniques in SNOBOL4, but much of the material has applicability to programming in general.

## 8.1 PROGRAM ORGANIZATION AND STRUCTURE

A SNOBOL4 program is simply a sequence of statements. From a logical point of view, however, programs can be divided into sections according to the nature of the operations performed or when these operations occur. Most programs have three distinct phases:

(a) initialization
(b) main processing
(c) termination

Typically, the initialization phase establishes the values of constants, creates patterns for later use, defines functions, assigns values to keywords, and so on. Following the main processing performed by a program, there is often, but not always, a termination phase in which final results are printed out. In planning a program, one of the first considerations should be what these phases will include. Special attention should be given to initialization, making sure that all variables have correct initial values and that program modes, such as anchored pattern matching, are properly established.

### Program Components

The division of a program into phases reflects a chronological point of view. More significant, however, is the division of a program into its logical parts. The key to writing a large program successfully is to organize the large program into a number of small sub-programs. The more independent, self-contained, and logically distinct these small sub-programs are, the more likely it is that the overall result will be good. A large program can, of course, be approached simply as a large number of statements to be written. The resulting organizational complexity and confusion may become insurmountable, however.

The main aid to subdivision of a program is the use of functions. By their nature, functions tend to be logically independent and self-contained. Therefore if the solution to a problem can be formulated in functional terms, the resulting program is likely to have good organization.

Formulating a solution in functional terms is a way of thinking and a matter of practice. For example, the word-counting problem may be thought of in terms of several functions:

| | |
|---|---|
| GETW | get a word |
| COUNT | count the word |
| PRINT | print results |

With this basic sketch of the solution, the beginning of a program can be laid out:

```
NEXTW   WORD   =   GETW()                        :F(DONE)

        COUNT(WCOUNT,WORD)                       :(NEXTW)

DONE    PRINT(WCOUNT)

END
```

This much of the program can be formulated without writing the procedures for the functions or even knowing exactly how they work. All that is necessary is to determine what basic operation each function performs. In the example above, GETW returns a word every time it is called. If a data file is being read, then GETW reads that file, and prints it if that is desired. Furthermore, GETW fails when there are no more words. COUNT counts the words, using a table. PRINT performs a well-defined operation and the details can be left until later.

Continuing with the development of this program, the initialization phase may be written next. It provides defining statements for the functions and creates needed structures. The need for a pattern to match words can be recognized at this point. A table to be used for word counting must be created also. Initialization statements therefore might be:

```
        LETTER  =   'ABCDEFGHIJKLMNOPQRSTUVWXYZ'

        WPAT  =  BREAK(LETTER) SPAN(LETTER) . GETW

        WCOUNT  =   TABLE()

        DEFINE('GETW()')

        DEFINE('COUNT(TABLE,STRING)')

        DEFINE('PRINT(TABLE)')
```

All that remains is to write the procedures themselves. These can be approached separately. For example, GETW finds the next word in a line of text, deletes it, and returns the word as value. If there are no more words in the line, however, GETW reads another line, prints it, and then returns the first word from the new line. When the data file is exhausted, there are no more words and therefore GETW fails.

Word counting is trivial, and printing the results is a matter of formatting. A complete program follows. Notice that the local variables ARRAY and I have been added for PRINT.

```
        LETTER   =    'ABCDEFGHIJKLMNOPQRSTUVWXYZ'

        WPAT   =    BREAK(LETTER) SPAN(LETTER) . GETW

        WCOUNT   =    TABLE()

        DEFINE('GETW()')

        DEFINE('COUNT(TABLE,STRING)')

        DEFINE('PRINT(TABLE)ARRAY,I')

NEXTW   WORD   =   GETW()                               :F(DONE)

        COUNT(WCOUNT,WORD)                              :(NEXTW)

DONE    PRINT(WCOUNT)                                   :(END)

GETW    LINE   WPAT   =                                 :S(RETURN)
```

```
        LINE   =   INPUT                                :F(FRETURN)
        OUTPUT   =   LINE                               :(GETW)
COUNT   TABLE<STRING>   =   TABLE<STRING> + 1           :(RETURN)
PRINT   OUTPUT   =
        ARRAY   =   CONVERT(TABLE,'ARRAY')              :F(NONE)
        I   =   1
RESULT  OUTPUT   =   ARRAY<I,1> ' - ' ARRAY<I,2>        :F(RETURN)
        I   =   I + 1                                   :(RESULT)
NONE    OUTPUT   =   'THERE ARE NONE'                   :(RETURN)
END
```

The example above is included to illustrate a technique. The problem itself is so simple that an elaborate solution of this kind is unnecessary. A solution without functions is given in Section 6.2. However, as a general method, such an approach divides the problem into its logical components and in doing so divides the solution into parts of manageable size. When such an approach is used, some functions, such as COUNT, may be so simple that they can be discarded in favor of a statement or two at the appropriate place in the program. The approach is the same, however.

Separating a program into functional components often has the additional advantage of producing functions that can be used in other programs. Thus, repetitious programming can be avoided. In the program above, for example, GETW is logically independent of the word-counting problem itself. Thus GETW might be useful in a variety of programs that deal with words taken from a data file. PRINT might be used as a general method of displaying the contents of a table. For this reason, the table is given as an argument of PRINT, even though that is unnecessary in the program above.

Patterns also can be used to divide the effort of programming into logical parts. Thus, in GETW a pattern WPAT is used, but WPAT is not given explicitly; instead it is created in the initialization phase. It is often useful when writing a pattern-matching statement to use a name for the pattern and write the pattern itself later. The advantage of doing this is that the process of writing statements does not have to be interrupted to develop a pattern. Patterns can be quite complicated and difficult to write. Simply providing a name avoids the distraction of having to write the pattern at that time. In this sense, a named pattern is like a function, and writing the pattern itself is like writing the procedure for a function. In order to treat patterns in this way, it is necessary to have a feeling for what can be done in a single pattern-matching statement. This understanding comes with experience.

### Program Evolution

Most programs of substantial size evolve over a period of time and are never really complete or stable. Rarely is a problem so well defined that every detail falls into place, every situation is considered, and no changes are subsequently made. More frequently the problem changes before the program solution is complete. In fact the problem is likely to change *after* the solution is thought to be complete. The major reason for such changes is the effect of the program itself. The process of reducing a problem to a program solution points out things that should be changed. Quite frequently results obtained from running a program suggest improvements, show errors in formulation, and almost always point out need for additions.

Since this is the case, a program is best thought of as an evolving entity. Change should be anticipated. As a program changes and modifications are made, the organization of the program may become more confused. An accumulation of minor changes may add unexpected complexity to otherwise simple operations. Corrections and modifications may make the program logic increasingly obscure. For this reason, good organizational design in the early stages of program development is essential. So long as the components can be kept independent, one part of the program can be rewritten without destroying the rest. The procedure for a function often can be completely rewritten without affecting the rest of the program, provided the operation the function is to perform is clearly defined and does not depend on other parts of the program.

Even with the best of intentions on the part of the programmer, a program may turn out to be inflexible and maddeningly difficult to modify or extend. Since a great amount of effort may go into a program over a period of time, there is an understandable resistance to discarding what has been done and starting over. Actually, however, much of the effort that is put into developing a large program is really a part of the problem-solving process. A program is the physical evidence of a much larger intellectual effort, and this effort is not wasted simply because a program is discarded to start anew on a better solution. Actually, there is often less effort involved in rebuilding a program than there is in trying to make modifications and extensions to a program that has outlived its usefulness. Therefore expect that the first attempts of a large programming problem will have to be discarded.

### Documentation

Commentary, program description, and instructions for program use are an important part of preparing a complete program. Program documentation is necessary because programs themselves usually are far from self-explanatory. Furthermore, program documentation may be required for users of the program. Documentation may help someone else to understand an algorithm or a technique which may then be useful in writing another program. Finally, documentation may be an important aid to the program's author.

A few weeks or months after a program is written, much may be forgotten. When corrections or modifications are needed, adequate documentation may save hours of painstaking work that would otherwise be spent trying to reconstruct the method from lines of program that suddenly seem meaningless.

The kind of documentation that is needed depends on the situation. The programs given in this book, for example, are described in the text and hence do not have documentation within them. Very short programs may be largely self-explanatory and may require little or no documentation. Large programs should always have documentation. The nature of the documentation depends on the use to which the program is to be put. Large programs used by many individuals, for example, may require user manuals. The concern in this section, however, is with self-contained documentation, documentation that is part of the program itself. Self-contained documentation, independent of any other documentation, is important since it is always available for reference in the program itself and cannot accidentally be lost or confused with documentation for another, similar program.

Documentation in a program may serve many purposes. The usual ones are:

(a) description of the purpose of the program.

(b) explanation of algorithms used.

(c) description of data required by the program; files used, data format, and so forth.

(d) description of the output produced, including any diagnostic messages.

(e) listing of any limitations the program is known to have.

(f) explanation of programming techniques used, especially anything unusual or obscure.

(g) suggestions for methods of extending the program to handle additional cases.

The most obvious form of self-contained documentation in a SNOBOL4 program is the comment line. A line beginning with an asterisk is ignored during execution of the program and, therefore, is the usual place to put documentation. The format and content of documentation is somewhat a matter of taste. No two programmers can be expected to produce the same documentation just as no two authors could be expected to write the same poem. Generally speaking, however, it is desirable to prepare the documentation in a format that is most likely to be useful and easily understood. A section of comment lines at the beginning of a program, summarizing the overall function and structure of the program, is usually a good choice. As an example, the word-counting program given earlier in this section might be preceded by the following comment lines:

```
*  THIS PROGRAM COUNTS THE NUMBER OF TIMES EACH WORD
*  OCCURS IN TEXT WHICH IS READ IN FROM A DATA FILE.
*
*  THE DATA FILE MUST BE PREPARED SO THAT NO WORD IS SPLIT
*  BETWEEN TWO RECORDS.  WORDS ARE ASSUMED TO CONSIST OF
*  STRINGS OF LETTERS.  A MORE SOPHISTICATED DEFINITION
*  OF WORDS COULD BE PROVIDED TO IMPROVE THE PROGRAM.
*
*  THE PROGRAM USES THREE FUNCTIONS:  GETW, COUNT, AND
*  PRINT TO GET THE WORDS, COUNT THEM, AND PRINT THE
*  RESULTS, RESPECTIVELY.  A TABLE IS USED TO REFERENCE
*  THE WORDS AND CONTAIN THE COUNTS
```

Obscure operations or nonobvious situations, especially if they are isolated instances, should have accompanying comment lines. An example is given by the GETW procedure:

```
*  LINE IS A GLOBAL VARIABLE CONTAINING THE REMAINDER OF
*  AN INPUT RECORD THAT HAS NOT BEEN PROCESSED.  WHEN GETW
*  IS FIRST CALLED, THE VALUE OF LINE IS NULL.  THEREFORE
*  THE FIRST PATTERN MATCH FAILS.  AS A RESULT, A RECORD
*  IS READ.  HENCE GETW IS SELF-INITIALIZING.
*
GETW  LINE  WPAT  =                          :S(RETURN)
      LINE  =  INPUT                         :F(FRETURN)
      OUTPUT  =  LINE                        :(GETW)
```

Avoid unnecessary or trivial comments. Consider the following lines:

```
*        INCREMENT THE VALUE OF I

         I    =    I + 1
```

The comment is pointless and distracting since the statement itself is obvious.

The example above leads to another aspect of documentation that is often overlooked. Ideally, programs should be self-documenting in the sense that the operations themselves should be as clear as a narrative description. Unfortunately no programming language is really self-documenting in this sense, although some are better than others. In SNOBOL4, some operations, such as the one shown in the example above, are obvious, while others (particularly pattern matching) are often obscure. Nevertheless, the program itself can often be written in a way that will enhance its self-documenting properties.

One principle that may be applied toward this goal is avoiding obscure and tricky techniques if a straightforward method is available. Programmers often get intellectual excitement and amusement from using obscure techniques. The reason given for this type of programming often is that the resulting program is more efficient. Actually such programs are usually inferior when viewed from a more general standpoint. An obscure and tricky program is difficult to understand, modify, and correct.

A technique that can be used to improve the self-documenting properties of a program is the choice of good mnemonics for names and labels. The particular characters chosen have no meaning to SNOBOL4, but if they are chosen to be suggestive of the operation involved, they can be a considerable help in making the program understandable to programmers and users. The following program is an example of the effect of lack of mnemonic value.

```
        N1   =   'ABCDEFGHIJKLMNOPQRSTUVWXYZ'

        N2   =   BREAK(N1) SPAN(N1) . F1

        N4   =   TABLE()

        DEFINE('F1()')

        DEFINE('F2(A1,A2)')

        DEFINE('F3(A1)L1,L2')

 L1     N5   =   F1()                                :F(L2)

        F2(N4,N5)                                    :(L1)

 L2     F3(N4)                                       :(END)
```

```
F1      N6    N2     =                              :S(RETURN)
        N6    =    INPUT                            :F(FRETURN)
        OUTPUT   =    N6                            :(F1)
F2      A1<A2>   =    A1<A2> + 1                    :(RETURN)
F3      OUTPUT   =
        L1    =    CONVERT(A1,'ARRAY')              :F(L4)
        L2    =    1
L3      OUTPUT   =    L1<L2,1> ' - ' L1<L2,2>       :F(RETURN)
        L2    =    L2 + 1                           :(L3)
L4      OUTPUT   =    'THERE ARE NONE'              :(RETURN)
END
```

This program is simply a translation of the word-counting program given earlier, using arbitrary names and labels.

The layout of a program is another important matter. Good layout involves: (a) a good correspondence between the logical organization and physical organization of the program, and (b) a choice of a readable format for the statements themselves. The logical organization of a program is usually clearer if the initialization section is first, the main processing section second, and the termination section last. Similarly, function procedures are usually best grouped together in one place. In general, similar and related operations should be physically adjacent where possible.

SNOBOL4 provides a great deal of flexibility in the way that statements are actually written. For example, the number of blanks used between components is left to the discretion of the programmer. Several statements may be given on a single line, and statements may be continued on several lines. A program is usually easier to read, however, if the parts of a statement are put in fixed positions. In the programs given in this book, for example, most subjects of statements start in the same column, and, so far as possible, gotos are arranged in a column. Similarly, equal signs are surrounded by more blanks than are used to surround operators. This makes the grouping of components easier to determine. Different programmers have different preferences for formatting statements. Formatting is largely a matter of taste; consistency is important.

To illustrate how difficult it is to understand a program that is not laid out in a readable way, consider the following example.

```
 LETTER = 'ABCDEFGHIJKLMNOPQRSTUVWXYZ'; WPAT = BREAK(LETTER)
+ SPAN(LETTER) . GETW; WCOUNT = TABLE(); DEFINE('GETW()')
  DEFINE('COUNT(TABLE,STRING)'); DEFINE('PRINT(TABLE)ARRAY,I')
NEXTW WORD = GETW() :F(DONE); COUNT(WCOUNT,WORD) :(NEXTW)
DONE PRINT(WCOUNT) :(END);GETW LINE WPAT = :S(RETURN); LINE
+ = INPUT :F(FRETURN); OUTPUT = LINE :(GETW);COUNT
+ TABLE<STRING> = TABLE<STRING> + 1 :(RETURN);PRINT OUTPUT =
 ARRAY = CONVERT(TABLE,'ARRAY') :F(NONE); I = 1;RESULT
+ OUTPUT = ARRAY<I,1> ' - ' ARRAY<I,2> :F(RETURN); I = I + 1
+ :(RESULT);NONE OUTPUT = 'THERE ARE NONE' :(RETURN);END
```

This is, again, the word-counting program given earlier, reformatted to fit on as few lines as possible. The result requires considerably fewer lines, which is useful for some purposes, but it is hardly a form that can be easily understood or modified.

## 8.2 REPRESENTATION OF DATA

Representation of data for computing processing is one of the most important and at the same time one of the most vexing aspects of programming. There are usually many alternative forms of representation. The factors that influence the selection of a specific form are often complex and frequently misunderstood, since there are many aspects of data representation and relatively few rigorous standards to apply. Intuition and good aesthetic judgement are most helpful. Some considerations in representing data for computer processing have general applicability. These are considered first, followed by considerations that apply specifically to SNOBOL4.

Data usually exists in three phases during computer processing:

(1) input data
(2) internal data
(3) output data

Usually the representation of data in different phases is different, although that need not be the case. Sometimes data has several different representations in one phase.

Input data is necessarily represented as strings in some way, because strings are the only form of data that can be read into a program. The range of internal representations is far richer, however. SNOBOL4 provides strings, numbers, arrays, tables, and programmer-defined data objects. The ways that these representations of data can be used are endless in their variety. Ultimately the results must be output, and again the constraint to strings applies. Figure 8.1 illustrates this situation schematically.

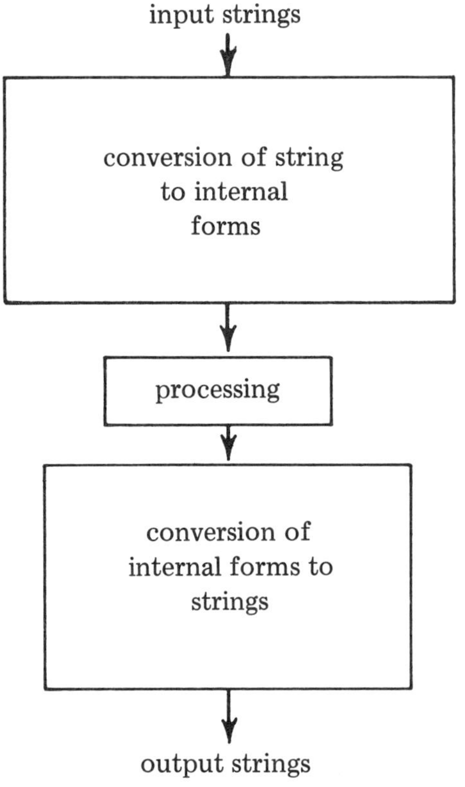


**Figure 8.1** Conversion of Data Forms

Because of the greater constraints on external representations of data, the problem of data representation is divided into two parts: string representations and internal representations.

### Considerations in String Representations

Any data that can be processed by a SNOBOL4 program can be represented by strings. However, certain considerations must be made when data is prepared for a specific computer, and some general constraints apply to choosing formats for data that is to be processed by a program. Printed and written data, whether it be mathematical equations, musical scores, or text, is usually represented by symbols arranged in two dimensions on a page.

In simple cases, the number of different symbols required is small and the structure of the data is sufficiently simple that vertical excursions are unnecessary. Hence the data can simply be represented as a sequence of lines. A page of text in a nontechnical book is an example. If the relationships between parts of the data are more complex, vertical offsets are usually used. An example is the following equation.

$$x^2 + y^2 - 6x - 10y + 18 = 0$$

This equation uses symbols in two sizes and also uses superscripting (i.e., an offset in the vertical direction). Computer input is, in almost all cases, constrained to be in a linear format and is made up from a relatively small character set. Thus, data to be manipulated by a program often must be prepared in an awkward and sometimes unreadable format with various techniques employed to represent unavailable characters.

Character sets vary considerably from machine to machine. Older machines typically allow only 64 different characters and lack lower-case letters. Most newer machines have 128 or 256 characters and include lower-case letters and a number of useful special characters. Obviously it is more pleasant, when manipulating strings, to work on a machine with a large character set. In such cases, textual data can often be represented almost exactly as it appears in print. If lower-case letters are not available, however, only an approximation of textual data can be represented.

Even if a computer has a large character set, the device that is used to prepare the data may not. For example, the standard keypunch machine does not have lower-case letters. Similarly most computer printers are incapable of printing the entire character set of a machine. On the other hand, many installations now offer computer terminals with keyboards similar to those of typewriters, and the character set of these terminals is large enough to comfortably accommodate most situations.

When representing data as strings, it is desirable, where possible, to have the individual datum represented as a single character. This is often quite natural to do. For example, the arithmetic operators usually are represented by the symbols `+`, `-`, `*`, and `/`. Such a representation is desirable since there are a number of functions that operate on individual characters. `REPLACE` is one. The pattern-valued functions `ANY`, `BREAK`, `NOTANY`, and `SPAN` are others. Similarly, if a character is known to exist in a given position, it can be matched by `LEN(1)`. Operations that locate one of a number of single characters are therefore easy to program, and run efficiently. The example of arithmetic operators given above illustrates where a choice may be made. In SNOBOL4, the exponentiation operator can be written in two ways: `**` and `!`. If the exponentiation operator is to be included in data, it is more desirable to have it represented by the single character `!`, making all operators coordinate in their representation and permitting them to be treated in the same way during processing. If `**` is used, on the other hand, an exception for exponentiation must be made whenever operator symbols are processed.

The equation given earlier can be represented as a string of characters so that it can be used as input data to a program. To do that, some modifications have to be made.

Upper-case letters can be used instead of lower-case letters with little loss of meaning. The superscripts indicate exponentiation, which can be written explicitly. The operation of multiplication is implied in the terms $6x$ and $10y$. For program processing, it is usually better to represent such implied operations explicitly to avoid ambiguity. Thus this equation might be represented by the string:

```
X!2+Y!2-6*X-10*Y+18=0
```

Generally speaking, almost all preparation of data involves some encoding of symbols. In the case of text, the encoding may consist simply of substituting upper-case letters for lower-case letters. For more complicated and structured types of data, more elaborate coding is required. Since data varies so widely, no general rules can be given. Some considerations are:

(a) ease and cost of preparing data in the encoded form
(b) ease of correction of encoded data
(c) readability of encoded data
(d) efficiency of processing encoded data
(e) ease of programming manipulation of encoded data

The relative importance that should be attached to these factors depends on circumstances. It is worthwhile to perform some tests using a chosen encoding method before making a commitment to that particular method. If a large amount of data must be encoded, the cost and the likelihood that errors may be introduced in the encoding process should be given major consideration. Fortunately SNOBOL4 is well-suited to converting data from one form of encoding to another. If a poor method is chosen initially, a SNOBOL4 program can often be written with little effort to convert the data to a better format.

Output of data also requires choosing a suitable string representation. Output is usually done for one of two purposes: to obtain a printed output for displaying results, or to obtain a punched output for input to another program. If the output is to provide input to another program, then the same considerations apply in a choice of a string representation for output as apply for input.

Most output, however, is designed to display results. In the initial stages of program development, the form of output may be crude. Eventually, however, some care needs to be taken to present the results in an easily read and attractive format. This consideration is especially applicable when the results are to be read by someone other than the programmer. The preparation of well-formatted printed output is a difficult and tedious job. Simply choosing the format requires perspective — an understanding of how it will look to someone who may not understand the program at all. Getting the printout in the desired format may become a substantial job. One facility available is carriage control in output formats. Thus an output association may be established to cause page ejection and titling. Arranging data in columns requires construction of suitable strings. The built-in function DUPL can be helpful in providing dividing lines or the appropriate number of blanks to separate data in columns.

### Internal Representations

While data must be read in and put out as strings, there are a variety of internal representations that may be used. If the data is naturally represented as a string, there may be no necessity for working with a different internal representation. Mathematical expressions and short sections of text are often most easily and naturally handled as strings in the same format as they are read in and put out.

If the amount of data is large, or if there are obvious or implied structural relationships among parts of the data, a string representation is probably not appropriate. In such cases, the relationships among parts of the data and the type of operations to be performed should govern the choice of a representation. Usually different representations have good and bad aspects, and any choice is a compromise.

A list of words provides an example. One way to represent a list is simply as a string in which the words are followed by commas. Such a representation is illustrated by:

```
WLIST   =   'YOU,CAN,FOOL,SOME,OF,THE,PEOPLE,'
```

For some purposes, such a string representation might be convenient. For other purposes, it would be awkward. For example, a word can easily be added to the end of WLIST, but it is difficult to obtain a particular word from a list represented in this form. If processing requires that words be accessed according to their position in the list, then an array of words may be more desirable. In such a representation, WLIST might be an array in which the subscripts would reference words. An example is

```
WLIST<1>   =   'YOU'

WLIST<2>   =   'CAN'

WLIST<3>   =   'FOOL'

               •

               •

               •
```

On the other hand, arrays are fixed in length and if the number of words is unknown or varying, that may present difficulties.

Different problems arise if there is a value associated with each word on a list. In the string representation, two corresponding lists, containing words and values respectively, could be used. In the array representation, a second dimension might be used so that the words and their corresponding values could be kept in the same structure.

If it is necessary to find the value associated with a particular word, neither the string nor the array representation is convenient. In this case a table may provide the best representation. Refer to Sections 6.1, 6.2, and the exercises at the end of this chapter.

In cases where there is a collection of similar objects, all having the same attributes or properties, a defined data object is appropriate. More elaborate structures also can be built up using defined data types. These structures in turn may be used to represent more complex relationships among data.

## 8.3 EFFICIENCY

Efficiency is the subject of much concern in programming. The reason is simple: the efficiency with which a program runs is directly related to cost. Since computers are expensive, the amount of computer time required to run a program is a valid consideration in measuring the quality and value of that program. Speed is not the only problem. The amount of memory that a program uses is often a factor in the cost of running it.

Ideally a program should run as fast as possible and should use as little memory as possible. Unfortunately these two goals are often in conflict. Quite frequently one technique will make a program run faster but use more memory, while another technique will have the opposite effect.

There are other considerations that relate to cost. One consideration is the cost of programming. Another is the importance of a well-organized and flexible program. Very often a program can be made to run more efficiently through the use of obscure techniques, clever shortcuts, and tricks. The result may be incomprehensible, difficult to correct, and virutally impossible to modify when changes or additions are desired. Good programming requires an intelligent balance among contending factors.

The greatest sources of inefficiency are poor algorithms, poor program organization, and poor data representation. Even if an efficient algorithm has been developed, a good data representation has been chosen, and the program has been laid out well, there remain questions of how best to perform individual operations. In SNOBOL4, the fastest technique, or the one that uses the least space, cannot be determined simply by a knowledge of what operations are performed by different language features. Determining the time required to perform an operation or the space required to represent a data object requires an understanding of the internal structure of SNOBOL4 and how it relates to what actually goes on in a computer. This understanding requires considerable background and study, and is beyond the experience of most programmers. The reader who is interested in such matters may consult Reference 4. In fact such knowledge should not be required in order to program, and too great a preoccupation with such matters interferes with the process of programming.

The following paragraphs state some good and bad practices in SNOBOL4. Some are common sense. There are others which are, for the most part, related to the internal structure of SNOBOL4. The latter may be taken on faith without having to have the detailed knowledge which would explain the reasons. The internal workings vary somewhat depending on the particular computer and SNOBOL4 translator used. The suggestions that follow apply to the most generally available versions of SNOBOL4. See References 1 and 4 for details.

1. Generally speaking, use as few statements as possible to perform an operation. There is some overhead associated with executing a statement. If operations can be logically combined in a statement, for example an assignment that is conditional upon a predicate, the result will be faster than separate statements. The overhead is relatively small, however, and statements should not be made so complicated that their meaning is obscured.

2. Avoid the use of very long strings. While SNOBOL4 permits string to be so long that length is usually not a physical limitation, operations on long strings can be very time-consuming. Therefore as a general rule, strings of over a few hundred characters should be avoided. In particular, never try to represent a long passage of text as a single string. If a large amount of data must be processed, organize the program to do it line by line so that input records can be processed and then discarded.

3. Perform input in the trimming mode if possible. The resulting strings read in are shorter and hence occupy less space. For this purpose, use &TRIM rather than the built-in function TRIM.

4. Use predicates where possible, rather than pattern matching. Predicates provide a fast and natural way for comparing data objects. Pattern matching can often be used to obtain the same result, but it is slower. For example, the following two statements do the same thing:

   ```
   IDENT(SWITCH,'YES')                          :S(OKAY)F(RETRY)

   SWITCH   POS(0) 'YES' RPOS(0)                :S(OKAY)F(RETRY)
   ```

   The first statement is better.

5. Perform pattern matching in the anchored mode if possible. Often a program can be easily written to run in the anchored mode. This is desirable because pattern matching can be time-consuming. When a pattern fails to match, much time can be spent in trying alternatives needlessly. Often, this wasted time can be avoided by using anchored matching so that failure occurs at once if the pattern cannot match starting at the first character of the subject string. If most of the program can be written to run in the anchored mode, but a few statements cannot, it may be worthwhile to turn the anchored mode on and off for different parts of the program. Alternatively, ARB can be placed at the beginning of patterns that will not work properly in the anchored mode.

6. Use the character-set patterns created by ANY, BREAK, NOTANY, and SPAN in preference to other patterns. The character-set patterns are generally faster than other patterns. In particular, the use of ANY is much more desirable than the alternation of single characters if many characters are involved. The pattern resulting from ANY is faster and smaller.

7. Avoid constructing a complicated pattern in the statement in which it is used for pattern matching. Patterns are data objects, require time for construction, and occupy space. If a pattern is given explicitly in a statement, that pattern is constructed every time that statement is executed. Therefore it is desirable to construct patterns at the beginning of program execution, assign them to names, and then refer to them by their names when needed in pattern matching. Thus the statement

```
NEXTAD LINE    BAL . L ANY('+-') BAL . R
```

might better be replaced by:

```
          ADDOP    =    BAL . L ANY('+-') BAL . R

                   .

                   .

                   .

NEXTAD LINE    ADDOP
```

8. Use arrays rather than tables where appropriate. Arrays require less space than tables, and array references are faster than table references. Although tables can have numerical subscripts, use arrays instead of tables if numerical subscripts are used to access a collection of data objects. On the other hand, if data objects must be accessed by their values, tables are preferable to other programming techniques that achieve the same effect.

9. Indirect referencing is a fast operation; do not hesitate to use it when it is appropriate.

### Programs that Require a Large Amount of Space

Sometimes space becomes more of a problem than just cost; there may not be enough memory space available to run a program. When this circumstance occurs, special programming techniques may have to be employed. Some suggestions follow:

1. Make the program as small as possible. The program itself occupies space. If the program is very long, that space may be quite significant. Avoid repetitious sections of program. A defined function can often be used to consolidate similar operations in one place. Similarly, patterns that are identical should appear only once and should be assigned to a name which is then used in several places.

2. Avoid programs that require keeping a large amount of data in memory at the same time. No matter how much memory space is available, there is always some upper limit. For example, there is no hope of running a program that requires the entire text of a

book to be in memory at the same time. Generally speaking, it is best to arrange a program to process data in small sections. This type of program organization is sometimes more difficult, but it is necessary in many cases. In other cases, such problems can be overcome by writing intermediate data on a file for subsequent processing later in the program. If nothing else solves the problem, divide the program into several programs that run consecutively. If this is done, intermediate programs may punch data or write it on files for use of subsequent programs.

3. Avoid a large number of different strings. There is some extra space required for each different string. This applies to strings that appear in the program as well as those created when the program runs. The same string can be used as a data string, a name, and a label. As such, it occurs only once in memory. Therefore using the same string for a label and a name (as is done in defined functions) can result in a saving of space.

4. Keep numerical values as numbers, not numeral strings. Integers and real numbers occupy less space than numeral strings having the same value. If many numerical values have to be kept, this consideration may be quite important. Numeral strings typically result from data that is read in, since numerical operations produce numbers, not numeral strings. A simple device may be used to convert a numeral string to a number: the unary plus operator. This operator does not change the numerical value of its operand, but does produce a number. Therefore to obtain a number from a data file, the following statement might be used:

```
      N    =    +TRIM(INPUT)                              :F(EOF)
```

## EXERCISES

**8.1.** A concordance is a citation of the places where words occur in text. Concordances have various forms, some of which are quite elaborate. A simple form of concordance is the index concordance which simply lists the lines in which each word in a text occurs. Using the method described in Section 8.1, develop an indexing program.

**8.2.** Write two functions LPAD(S,N) and RPAD(S,N) that pad S with blanks on the left and right respectively to produce strings N characters long. Using the results, redo Exercise 3.4.

**8.3.** Suppose that a list of words is represented by a string as described in Section 8.2. Write a function GETW(WLIST,N) whose value is the Nth word in WLIST. Compare this function with the method for accessing a list of words in an array.

**8.4.** Suppose that a list of words and corresponding counts is represented by a two-dimensional array WCOUNT. Write a function GETC(WCOUNT,WORD) whose value is the count for WORD. Compare this function to the method for accessing the count of words in a table.

**8.5.** Suppose that a list of words is to be read from a data file and placed in an array for processing.

(a) Design a format for the data so that placing words in the array is easy to program.

(b) Design a format for the data to minimize the number of data records required.

Write programs to read the data and construct the array for both cases. Assume that there will be no more than 100 words. Discuss the advantages and disadvantages of each data format.

**8.6.** Write programs to convert data between the formats developed in the solution of Exercise 8.5.

**8.7.** In a list of words, commas are convenient separators. What can be used as a separator in a list of strings? Discuss the problems involved. Is there any general way to represent a list of strings as a string?

**8.8.** What general type of data representation is best for the following types of data?

(a) A checkerboard.

(b) An address list.

(c) A collection of archaeological objects.

(d) A table of contents for a book.

(e) A musical score.

CHAPTER 9

# Program Debugging

Almost all programs contain errors when they are first written. An exception is sometimes the first program that a person writes, since this crucial attempt is given unusual thought and care. After the first attempt, however, things change. This is not surprising or necessarily indicative of carelessness. Programs become large and complex. Very large programs, as a matter of fact, are almost never totally free of error.

Program errors are called *bugs* and the process of removing errors is called *debugging.* Bugs come in all sizes and shapes. Some are obvious after the first run, while others are subtle and elude detection. Some of the most elusive bugs occur in the handling of special cases. For example, a program that works properly in most cases may come apart altogether if the data on which it is supposed to operate is accidentally omitted. The most pervasive type of bug is the one that is dependent on the form of data. It is quite common for a program that has been working well for months or years to suddenly develop all sorts of bugs when it is given to another user. Usually the reason is that the new user has different data, data that the program was not properly designed to handle.

Program debugging is important because it occupies so much of a programmer's time and energy and consumes significant amounts of computer time. Good programming practices can go a long way toward preventing program bugs in the first place. No matter how excellent a programmer may be, however, his programs will have bugs. Furthermore there are some kinds of bugs that are most easily and economically found by running the program. The computer excels at clerical tasks, while human beings are notoriously poor clerks; therefore appropriate use of the computer to aid in debugging can be very valuable. It may seem expensive and wasteful to use a computer to find program errors, but human resources are expensive also—more so than is often realized. There is no economy in expending days of a highly skilled programmer's time trying to find an obscure program bug that could be pinpointed by a computer run of a few seconds. The programmer has intelligence while the computer has speed and clerical ability. The key in debugging is to utilize both programmer talent and the computer in appropriate ways so that debugging is swift and inexpensive.

## 9.1 PRINTED OUTPUT FROM A PROGRAM RUN

The main source of debugging information is the printed output from a computer run. When a SNOBOL4 program is run on a computer, it passes through three distinct phases. During the first of these phases, the program is processed by the SNOBOL4 system and put in a form suitable for execution by the computer. This phase is called *compilation.* When compilation is complete, the program is executed by the computer, carrying out the computations specified in the program. This phase is called *execution.* Finally there is a termination phase which follows execution. Typically each of these phases produces printed output.

### Compilation

The program is printed as it is compiled. Each statement is given an identifying number. If an error is detected in a statement during compilation, an error message is printed beneath the statement. This message describes the nature of the error. A marker indicates the approximate location of the error. Compilation is continued despite errors unless more than 50 errors are detected, in which case compilation is abandoned. At the end of compilation, a message is printed indicating whether or not any errors have been detected. A complete compilation listing follows, showing the form of the listing.

```
SNOBOL4 (VERSION 3.9,  MAY 19, 1972)

BELL TELEPHONE LABORATORIES, INCORPORATED



READ    CARD   =   INPUT                          :F(TERM)  1

        CARD   '*'                                :F(READ)  2

        COUNT  =   COUNT + 1                      :(READ)   3

TERM    OUTPUT  =   COUNT ' CONTAIN A STAR'                 4

END                                                         5

NO ERRORS DETECTED IN SOURCE PROGRAM
```

A compilation listing from a program containing two errors follows:

```
SNOBOL4 (VERSION 3.9,  MAY 19, 1972)

BELL TELEPHONE LABORATORIES, INCORPORATED

READ    CARD   =    INPUT                                    :F(TERM)     1

        CARD    TAB(10) ' '                                  :F(READ)     2

        COUNT   =     COUNT+1                                :(READ)      3

                      '

**** ILLEGAL CHARACTER IN ELEMENT

$ERM    OUTPUT   =    COUNT ' ARE CORRECT'                                4

'

**** ERRONEOUS LABEL

END                                                                       5

ERRORS DETECTED IN SOURCE PROGRAM
```

Errors that are detected during compilation are mainly syntactic ones. Semantic errors, i.e., errors of meaning, cannot be detected until the program is actually executed, if then. The errors in the second program above are typical and self-explanatory. The most common syntactic errors are listed in Section 9.4.

Since the SNOBOL4 system has no way of knowing what the programmer intends to do, the error detected may not be the error the programmer made but may have resulted only from an error earlier in the statement. Usually a little study will disclose the error and a few simple corrections will produce a program that compiles without further error. Only the first error in any statement is detected. Therefore an erroneous statement should be examined carefully to be sure it does not contain other errors.

### Execution

During execution of a program, printed output is produced by the program itself as a result of assignments to OUTPUT. Ordinarily the SNOBOL4 system does not print messages during execution, since such messages would be intermixed with the program output and might ruin the appearance of an otherwise satisfactory printout.

There are, however, tracing modes which may be used. When executing a program in a tracing mode, various messages about the progress of execution are provided automatically by the SNOBOL4 system. Tracing is described in Section 9.2.

### Termination

Program execution may be terminated by transferring to the label END or by flowing into the label END. When this occurs, a termination message is printed indicating that execution has ended normally. A typical message follows.

```
NORMAL TERMINATION AT LEVEL  0

LAST STATEMENT EXECUTED WAS     7
```

The level given is the level of call of programmer-defined functions. Usually the level is zero, but it may be greater than zero since it is possible to transfer to END while executing the procedure for a function.

If an error occurs during program execution, execution is terminated at that point and an appropriate message is printed. An example is:

```
ERROR 24 IN STATEMENT     6 AT LEVEL  0

UNDEFINED OR ERRONEOUS GOTO
```

Transfer to a label that does not occur in the program will produce error termination of the type indicated above. Each error has a number which can be looked up in the reference manual in case a lengthier explanation is needed.

Whatever the cause of termination, summary statistics are given at the end of the printed output. These statistics provide timing information and counts of certain operations that occurred during program execution. A typical set of summary statistics follows.

```
SNOBOL4 STATISTICS SUMMARY:

               81 MS. COMPILATION TIME
                4 MS. EXECUTION TIME
                6 STATEMENTS EXECUTED,      2 FAILED
                2 ARITHMETIC OPERATIONS PERFORMED
                3 PATTERN MATCHES PERFORMED
                0 READS PERFORMED
                1 WRITES PERFORMED
              .66 MS. AVERAGE PER STATEMENT EXECUTED
```

The abbreviation " MS " stands for milliseconds, i.e., thousandths of a second.

Sometimes the information provided in the statistics may be helpful in locating an error. For example, the program that produced the statistics above did not read any data records. This might indicate an error.

## 9.2 TRACING

Since most errors occur during program execution, diagnostic information about the course of program execution is an essential aid to debugging. The judicious placement of output statements can be helpful in this regard. In addition, the SNOBOL4 system itself can be placed in modes in which diagnostic information is provided automatically.

### The TRACE Mode

The TRACE mode is established by assigning a positive integer to the keyword &TRACE. An example is the statement:

```
        &TRACE   =   1000
```

The value assigned to &TRACE determines the extent of tracing output as is described later.

Turning on the trace mode does not cause tracing itself. Tracing to be done is determined by trace associations made with specific names. Such associations are made by the built-in function TRACE. An example is:

```
        TRACE('TEXT')
```

This statement specifies that the name TEXT is to be traced. If the trace mode is on (i.e., if the value of &TRACE is greater than zero), a trace message is printed every time a value is assigned to TEXT. Trace messages occur for assignments which are made as a result of replacement and as a result of names attached to patterns, as well as for simple assignment statements. Messages show what value is assigned to TEXT, in what statement the assignment was made, and when the assignment was made.

Consider the following program.

```
        &TRACE   =   1000

        TRACE('TEXT')

        VOWELS   =   SPAN('AEIOU')

        TEXT   =   'AFTERNOON SIESTAS'

REMOVE  TEXT   VOWELS   =   '-'                     :S(REMOVE)

END
```

Trace messages resulting from executing this program are:

```
STATEMENT 4: TEXT = 'AFTERNOON SIESTAS',TIME = 4

STATEMENT 5: TEXT = '-FTERNOON SIESTAS',TIME = 9

STATEMENT 5: TEXT = '-FT-RNOON SIESTAS',TIME = 14

STATEMENT 5: TEXT = '-FT-RN-N SIESTAS',TIME = 21

STATEMENT 5: TEXT = '-FT-RN-N S-STAS',TIME = 30

STATEMENT 5: TEXT = '-FT-RN-N S-ST-S',TIME = 40
```

The time printed is given in milliseconds measured from the beginning of program execution.

Each time a trace message is printed, the value of &TRACE is automatically decreased by one. When the value of &TRACE reaches zero, tracing turns off automatically. Thus

```
&TRACE   =   100
```

provides for 100 trace messages before tracing is turned off. Of course the value of &TRACE can be reset by an assignment statement at any time.

Several trace associations can be in effect at the same time. Each trace association is made by executing TRACE. For example, the statements

```
TRACE('VARIABLE')

TRACE('FORMULA')

TRACE('EXPRESSION')
```

establish trace associations for the three names VARIABLE, FORMULA, and EXPRESSION. Whenever a value is assigned to any of these variables, a trace message is printed. Each trace message identifies the name to which the assignment was made, and each trace message decrements the value of &TRACE.

Other program actions in addition to assignment may also be traced. Consult Reference 1 for a complete description of tracing.

### The FTRACE Mode

Another keyword, &FTRACE, permits tracing of programmer-defined functions. Function tracing is turned on by assigning a positive value to &FTRACE, as in the statement:

```
&FTRACE   =   1000
```

When function tracing is on, every call and return of a programmer-defined function produces a trace message. The information printed is similar to that printed when value assignments are traced.

Consider the following program.

```
        &FTRACE  =  100                                           1
        &ANCHOR  =  1                                             2
        &TRIM  =  1                                               3
        DEFINE('PRE(EXP)L,R,OP')                                  4
        INP  =  BAL . L ANY('+-/*') . OP BAL . R RPOS(0)          5
        RPAREN  =  POS(0)  '(' BAL . R ')' RPOS(0)                6
 READ   OUTPUT  =  INPUT                               :F(END)    7
        OUTPUT  =  PRE(OUTPUT)                                    8
        OUTPUT  =                                      :(READ)    9
 PRE    EXP  RPAREN  =  R                                         10
        EXP  INP  =  OP '(' PRE(L) ',' PRE(R) ')'                 11
        PRE  =  EXP                                    :(RETURN)  12
 END                                                              13
```

The printed output from execution of this program follows.

```
A+(B*C)

        STATEMENT 8: LEVEL 0 CALL OF PRE('A+(B*C)'),TIME = 18

        STATEMENT 11: LEVEL 1 CALL OF PRE('A'),TIME = 29

        STATEMENT 12: LEVEL 1 RETURN OF PRE = 'A',TIME = 35

        STATEMENT 11: LEVEL 1 CALL OF PRE('(B*C)'),TIME = 40

        STATEMENT 11: LEVEL 2 CALL OF PRE('B'),TIME = 53

        STATEMENT 12: LEVEL 2 RETURN OF PRE = 'B',TIME = 58
```

```
STATEMENT 11: LEVEL 2 CALL OF PRE('C'),TIME = 63

STATEMENT 12: LEVEL 2 RETURN OF PRE = 'C',TIME = 68

STATEMENT 12: LEVEL 1 RETURN OF PRE = '*(B,C)',TIME = 73

STATEMENT 12: LEVEL 0 RETURN OF PRE = '+(A,*(B,C))',TIME = 78

+(A,*(B,C))
```

## 9.3 OTHER DIAGNOSTIC INFORMATION

### Keywords

Additional information about the progress of program execution is available as the value of keywords. The value of the keyword &STCOUNT is a count of the number of statements that have been executed. The value of &STCOUNT is automatically incremented whenever execution of a statement is begun. Similarly &STFCOUNT contains a count of the number of statements that have failed. Printing out the values of these keywords at appropriate points during program execution may provide helpful information for debugging.

### Termination Dump

A listing of the values of names may be included in the information printed at program termination by assigning a positive integer to the keyword &DUMP. In the early stages of program debugging, it is advisable to include a statement such as:

```
        &DUMP   =   1
```

To obtain a dump, the particular integer assigned to &DUMP is irrelevant, so long as the value is positive. The dump that is provided lists all names that have nonnull values. A typical dump follows.

```
DUMP OF VARIABLES AT TERMINATION

ABORT = PATTERN

ARB = PATTERN

BAL = PATTERN

COUNT = 45
```

```
FAIL = PATTERN

FENCE = PATTERN

N = 8

OUTPUT = 'THERE ARE 45 SPECIAL CASES'

REM = PATTERN

SUCCEED = PATTERN

TEXT = 'SOME FORMS OF THE VERB ARE FOUND ONLY'
```

In such a dump, values that are not strings or numbers are indicated by their data types in the same way that such values are handled in printed output during execution. The dump above, for example, illustrates that ARB, BAL, and so forth have pattern values. It is important to remember that only names which have nonnull values are printed.

## 9.4 ERRORS

An endless variety of errors may be made in writing programs. Those that have to do with an incorrect method of solving a problem are beyond the scope of this book. Errors directly related to the use, or misuse, of SNOBOL4 are discussed in the following sections.

### Syntactic Errors

Errors in the formation of SNOBOL4 statements are called syntactic errors. Such errors are detected during the compilation phase of a SNOBOL4 run, and error messages are printed in the compilation listing. Some common mistakes are:

1. Failure to surround binary operators by blanks. This error is most frequently committed by programmers who are familiar with the syntax of another programming language (such as FORTRAN) which does not require blanks in the same places that SNOBOL4 does.
2. Failure to provide the closing quotation mark on a data string. A similar error occurs if an attempt is made to enclose a quotation mark in a data string which is delimited by that type of quotation mark. So far as the SNOBOL4 compiler is concerned, a data string begins when a quotation mark is encountered and ends when a corresponding quotation mark is found. Thus it is possible to "get out of synchronization" if a quotation mark is omitted in a statement containing several data strings.

3. Failure to match parentheses properly in nested expressions. Unlike quotation marks, parentheses can be nested. However, in complicated expressions, closing parentheses may be accidentally omitted, or too many closing parentheses may be provided. With a little practice, parentheses can be quickly counted using the method described in Section 4.2 for locating balanced strings.

Finally, it is important to understand that the SNOBOL4 compiler has no way of determining what a programmer meant to do. There are many syntactically correct programs that do not execute correctly. Consider the following example.

```
        OUTPUT    =    SIZE (S T)
```

This statement specifies a concatenation of the value of the name SIZE with the values of the names S and T. It is *not* a call of the function SIZE, which would be written:

```
        OUTPUT    =    SIZE(S T)
```

Both statements are syntactically correct, but they mean different things.

Programmers are sometimes surprised that a statement such as

```
        SIZE(X)    =    3
```

is syntactically correct, even though it is impossible to assign a value to a call of a built-in function. Observe, however, that if this statement is preceded by

```
        DATA('OBJECT(SIZE,LOCATION)')
```

then SIZE becomes a field function to which a value may be assigned. After executing DATA, SIZE is no longer a built-in function. Since SIZE can be redefined during execution, its appearance as the subject of an assignment is not a syntactic error.

### Error Messages During Execution

Since most errors cannot be detected during compilation, many errors become apparent during execution. Some errors simply cause the program to produce the wrong result and must be hunted by logical processes or the use of diagnostic information described in preceding sections. Other errors result in illegal operations which cause program termination with an error message. These error messages are generally self-explanatory. Examination of the statement in which the error occurred and the values of variables listed in the string dump usually pinpoints the mistake.

The commonest error messages and their most frequent causes are:

ILLEGAL DATA TYPE. This message is caused by an attempt to perform an operation on a type of object for which that operation is not defined. This is the commonest of all errors and its cause is usually an attempt to perform arithmetic on a nonnumerical object. A less obvious source of this error is an attempt to perform pattern matching on an object that is not a string. An example is:

```
        OPS     =    ANY('+-/*')

                .

                .

                .

        OPS     '+'                                         :S(PLUS)
```

The last statement is erroneous since the subject of the pattern match is a pattern, not a string. In this case, an examination of the string dump will show the data type of OPS is PATTERN.

ERROR IN ARITHMETIC OPERATION. The usual cause of this error is an attempt to divide by zero or to compute a result that is numerically larger than allowed.

NULL STRING IN ILLEGAL CONTEXT. While usually caused by an attempt to perform an indirect reference on the null string, this message also occurs if the argument of a field function is null. For example, if LSON is a field function as described in Section 6.3,

```
        LSON(X)    =    Y
```

produces the message above if the value of X is null. If the value of X is null, X will not be printed in the string dump. Hence its absence is a clue. An even more subtle source of this error message occurs when a null argument is given to one of the pattern-valued functions ANY, NOTANY, BREAK, or SPAN. An example is:

```
        DIGIT      =     '0123456789'

        INTEGER    =     SPAN(DIGITS)
```

The misspelling of DIGITS for DIGIT results in a null argument to SPAN.

UNDEFINED FUNCTION OR OPERATION. This message usually results from misspelling a function name or attempting to call a programmer-defined function before it has been defined.

VARIABLE NOT PRESENT WHERE REQUIRED. An attempt to assign a value to something that is not a variable causes this error. For example

```
        SIZE(X)    =    3
```

produces this error unless SIZE is appropriately redefined as, for example, a field function.

UNDEFINED OR ERRONEOUS GOTO. Usually this error is caused by an attempt to transfer to a label that is not in the program. Misspelling is the commonest source of such an error. Another cause of this error is specifying a value, rather than a name, in the goto field. This usually occurs in the case of a computed goto. To transfer to one of the labels L1, L2, L3, . . . the following goto is sometimes written:

```
                                                    :('L' N)
```

where N takes on different integer values. While this may look correct, it is an error. For example, to transfer to L3, one would write :(L3), not :('L3'). Thus, indirect referencing must be used to get the required name if the label is computed. The correct form for such a goto is:

```
                                                    :($('L' N))
```

This construction may not seem very natural and may be hard to understand, but it is required and becomes automatic with practice.

STACK OVERFLOW. This message indicates that an internal storage area, called the stack, has become full. This stack is used for saving information when programmer-defined functions are called. Stack overflow usually indicates runaway recursion in which a function is calling itself endlessly. Sometimes, however, a perfectly well-designed function can simply require more space on the stack than is available. In this case, the program may have to be redesigned.

INSUFFICIENT STORAGE TO CONTINUE. There is a main storage area that is used for holding the program and data objects created during execution. SNOBOL4 maintains this storage area, discarding unneeded objects when it is necessary to make space for new ones. The message above indicates that there is not enough space to continue running the program. This may be caused by a program that accidentally creates an endless number of objects that cannot be discarded. More often, this message indicates a program that really requires more space than is available. See Section 8.3 for a discussion of this problem.

### Some Nonobvious Errors

As was mentioned earlier, not all errors produce error messages; some errors simply cause the program to malfunction. Some nonobvious causes of program malfunction follow.

1. *Ambiguous failure.* Failure may occur for several reasons. If a statement may fail for more than one reason, the failure branch may produce misleading results. An example is:

```
         IPAIR   =   BREAK(',') . I1 ',' REM . I2

READ     INPUT   IPAIR                                   :F(DONE)
```

Here the failure exit is intended to indicate that all data has been read. If the data is not in the form expected, however, the statement may fail because the pattern fails to match. In such cases, two statements should be provided:

```
READ    LINE   =   INPUT                              :F(DONE)

        LINE   IPAIR                                  :F(ERROR)
```

2. *Unexpected failure.* Failure that is not expected is akin to the ambiguous failure described above. Here, however, the result is that the failure goes undetected. The following statement illustrates such a case. Suppose the value of T is a table.

```
        A    =    CONVERT(T,'ARRAY')
```

Ordinarily such a statement succeeds and assigns an array to A. If, however, T contains only subscripts with null values, CONVERT fails. The result is that no array is assigned to A. This fact may go undetected until A is referenced as an array. Such a reference produces an error message, but the reference may not occur until long after CONVERT has failed, obscuring the real source of trouble. Similarly, REPLACE fails if its second and third arguments are of different lengths. Generally speaking, failure gotos should be provided as safety measures on all statements containing CONVERT and REPLACE.

3. *Troubles with arrays.* Sometimes the form of the first and second arguments of ARRAY causes confusion. For example

```
        A1   =    ARRAY('3,4')
```

creates a two-dimensional array in which all subscripts have initial null values. On the other hand,

```
        A2   =    ARRAY('3','4')
```

creates a one-dimensional array in which all subscripts have the string 4 as initial value. More subtle is the error in the following statement.

```
        A1<1>   =   X
```

Since A1 is a two-dimensional array, the omitted second subscript is assumed to be the null string. The null string is numerically equivalent to zero. Thus this statement is equivalent to:

```
        A1<1,0>    =    X
```

This statement fails since the second argument is out of range.

4. *Trailing blanks.* Trailing blanks resulting from input are sometimes the cause of mysterious errors. Consider the following statements.

```
READ    LINE   =    INPUT                                :F(DONE)

GETI    LINE   BREAK(',') . I1 ',' REM . I2              :F(ERROR)

TEST    GT(I2,I1)                                        :S(ELIM)
```

   Here data cards contain pairs of integers separated by commas. An error is likely to occur in the statement labeled TEST. Unless the input is trimmed of trailing blanks, the value assigned to I2 may contain many trailing blanks. Hence the first argument of the arithmetic comparison is not an integer. Printed output is of little help since the blanks are "invisible". This problem may be avoided by changing the pattern in the statement labeled GETI:

```
GETI    LINE BREAK(',') . I1 ',' BREAK(' ') . I2    :F(ERROR)
```

   The converse problem may arise, as illustrated by the following statements.

```
        &TRIM   =   1

READ    LINE   =   INPUT                                 :F(DONE)

GETI    LINE   BREAK(',') . I1 ',' BREAK(' ') . I2   :F(ERROR)
```

   Here the statement labeled GETI fails since trailing blanks have been removed and there is nothing for BREAK(' ') to match.

5. *Numbers and numeral strings.* In most instances numbers and numeral strings may be used interchangeably and without concern for the difference. In a few situations, numbers and numeral strings cannot be used interchangeably, and these situations may cause subtle errors. The predicates IDENT and DIFFER compare their arguments as objects, regardless of their numerical values. Therefore a statement such as

```
        IDENT(TRIM(INPUT),COUNT + 1)                     :F(NO)
```

   always fails since the first argument is a string resulting from input and the second argument is a number resulting from addition. Similarly, while an array subscript may be an integer or a numeral string representing that integer, the two types of subscripts are different if used to reference a table.

### Controlling Execution

One of the most annoying problems is a program that loops. It is trivial to write a series of statements that repeats indefinitely. There is no reason for doing this purposely, but it happens accidentally quite frequently. In the sample programs in Section 2.11, an example of such an error was given. The particular statements were:

```
AGAIN   TEXT   'S'                          :F(NO)

        COUNT  =   COUNT + 1                :(AGAIN)
```

This kind of bug has several unpleasant features. First, the results of executing the program are almost always useless. Consequently the loop is wasteful of computer time. Second, a loop is often hard to locate.

Loops are common errors and if there were no way to stop them, programs with loops would run endlessly. Therefore computer installations usually place a limit on the time a program is permitted to run. Generally the programmer can specify this limit himself for a particular run. If this time limit is exceeded, the run is terminated unceremoniously. When this occurs, there is usually no indication of what the SNOBOL4 program was doing at the time. Consequently there may be no evidence of the location of the loop, or even if there is one. Worst of all, printed output is often lost when a program is terminated for exceeding the time limit. This happens because output is often kept in *buffers* in the memory of the computer, and is only printed when the buffers become full. When a SNOBOL4 program goes through its termination phase, these buffers are emptied ("flushed"). Time limit termination simply stops the run, there is no termination phase, and buffers may not be flushed.

SNOBOL4 provides a way to avoid many of these problems by limiting the number of statements that may be executed in a single run. A count of statements is kept, and when the limit given by the value of the keyword &STLIMIT is exceeded, error termination occurs with an appropriate error message. The termination phase then provides the usual summary information which may aid in debugging. The initial, default value of &STLIMIT is 50000, but this limit may be changed. If a program is to perform a great amount of computation, the limit may have to be raised. For debugging purposes, it is often desirable to set the limit to a low value. A statement such as

```
        &STLIMIT   =   1000
```

is typical. The advantage of such a low limit lies in the probability that a loop may be present. In the early stages of program development, the number of statements to be executed should not be large in any event. Almost all runs, at this point, are for the purpose of finding errors, not for producing useful calculations. If a loop is present, it is usually easily identifiable from the information provided by the termination phase. At first, it may be difficult to decide what limit to set. With a little experience, the amount of computation that can be performed with a thousand or two thousand statements becomes clear. Furthermore, estimating the number of statements required for various computations is a good exercise in itself.

### Steps in Locating Errors

In many cases, when a program does not work properly, the error is obvious and is easily corrected. If the error is somewhat obscure, a programmer may jump to the conclusion that the SNOBOL4 translator is at fault—that the "system" made an error. While an error in SNOBOL4 itself is not impossible, it is quite unlikely. SNOBOL4 has been in use for many years and errors found in it have been corrected. As a starting point, assume the program, not SNOBOL4, is in error.

There are some routine steps that should be undertaken in debugging. While they seem obvious, they are so often overlooked that they are given here.

1. Check the listing for error messages. If parts of the program have not been run before, check for compilation errors as well as execution errors. Look for something obviously wrong in the listing of the program itself, such as a mispunched card that should have been discarded, but was not.
2. If execution terminated with an error message, check the message and the indicated location. First determine if the cause of the error is obvious or appears reasonable. If the cause is not immediately clear, check the dump of names and their values. First check for the values of names used in the erroneous statement and in statements leading up to the error.
3. If there is still nothing obvious, or if the run terminated normally, check the values of all variables in the dump, looking for something obviously out of place. Also check the summary statistics to see if the number of operations performed is reasonable.
4. If examination of the output listing does not reveal the cause of the error, recheck the logic of the program and work out some simple cases by hand. If the program has run correctly before, but now malfunctions, pay special attention to any recent changes, however minor they may be. Also consider the possibility that something different in the data may have uncovered a latent bug.
5. If an examination of the type described above does not reveal the error, add debugging statements to the program and rerun it to get more information. Debugging statements should be aimed at producing useful printed output, either by output statements or tracing. Do not hesitate to print a substantial amount of information. In some cases `&STLIMIT` may be useful in locating a loop or stopping execution in a desired section of the program.

## EXERCISES

**9.1.** The following statements all contain syntactic errors. Identify the errors and suggest corrections.

```
          EQ(SIZE(S),N))                              :S(OKAY)
          OUTPUT   =   'THE RESULT IS S ' AT TERMINATION'
```

```
        1A    =    INPUT

        N    =    LT(N,SIZE(M) N + 1                        :F(DONE)
```

**9.2.** In an initial debugging run, what keywords should be assigned values that are different from their default values?

**9.3.** Write a program to count the number of different words on a data file. Trace the words found and the count. Run this program on some typical data and observe the results.

**9.4.** Run the solution of Exercise 5.6 in the FTRACE mode. What insight does the printed output provide?

**9.5.** Consider the word-counting program given in Section 6.2. Estimate how many statements will be required to process a data file consisting of 10 80-character records. Assign a value to &STLIMIT to force termination if the number of statements executed is more than twice the expected number.

**9.6.** The following program is designed to convert expressions from infix form to prefix form.

```
        DEFINE('PRE(EXP)L,R,OP')

        INP    =    POS(0) BAL . L ANY('+-/*') . OP BAL . R
+               RPOS(0)

        RPAREN    =    POS(0)  '(' BAL . R ')' RPOS(0)

READ    OUTPUT    =    INPUT                               :F(END)

        OUTPUT    =    PRE(OUTPUT)

        OUTPUT    =                                        :(READ)

PRE     EXP    RPAREN    =    R

        EXP    INP    =    OP '(' PRE(L) ',' PRE(R) ')'

        PRE    =    EXP                                    :(RETURN)

END
```

The program does not work properly. Locate the cause of the error and show how to correct it.

APPENDIX A

# Rules of Syntax

Certain rules must be followed in writing SNOBOL4 programs. Rules concerning the structure of statements in a program are called rules of *syntax*. Syntax is not concerned with what things mean or with what happens when a program is executed, but only with form. These rules are given throughout the book, often by example. The following paragraphs summarize some of the more important aspects of the syntax of SNOBOL4 in an informal way. Only the parts of SNOBOL4 described in this book are included; a complete and more formal syntax is given in Reference 1.

### Names

Names may be as long as desired, but must fit on one line. The first character of a name must be a letter. The rest of the characters may be letters, digits, or periods.

### Numbers

Integers are composed of digits. The maximum number of digits is limited by the maximum value that an integer can have, which varies from machine to machine. Real numbers must begin with a digit and have a decimal point (period). More digits may follow the decimal point. The allowable size of real numbers also depends on the machine.

### Labels and Gotos

Labels may be as long as desired, but must fit on one line. The first character of a label must be a letter or a digit. Any characters except blanks or semicolons may follow the first character. A blank terminates the label, and a semicolon terminates the label and also the statement. Although most labels are names, labels may contain characters that are not allowable in names. Thus B⁘ is an acceptable label.

Most gotos contain names that are given explicitly. Indirect referencing may be used to compute a label, however. In this way control may be transferred to a statement whose label is not a name. The following statements illustrate this situation:

```
          OP    =    '⁘'
                .
                .
                .
                                                     :($('B' OP))
```

The goto constructs the string B⁘ which is then referenced indirectly to transfer control to the statement with the label B⁘. There is sometimes confusion about indirect referencing in gotos. The indirect reference is necessary in the statement above, since the result of concatenation is a data string. To transfer to the label B, the goto :(B) is used, not :('B').

### Use of Blanks

Blanks are used for a number of different purposes in SNOBOL4. One use is for separating the major components of a statement. Thus, blanks separate a label from a subject, a subject from a pattern, an equal sign from other components, and so on. Blanks are also required around binary operators to separate the operators from their operands. Finally, blanks indicate concatenation. In any of these uses, at least one blank is required, but as many more may be used as desired.

Because binary operators are surrounded by blanks and because blanks are used in concatenation, blanks must not be used between a function name and the parentheses enclosing the arguments, or after unary operators.

The use of blanks to separate components and also to indicate concatenation frequently causes confusion in determining the subject of a statement. Consider the following statement.

```
          X   Y  Z
```

This might be interpreted to be a pattern-matching statement in which the pattern is Z and the subject is the concatenation of X and Y. In fact, the blanks between the X and Y separate the subject from the pattern, which is Y concatenated with Z. Thus the statement above is equivalent to:

```
          X  (Y  Z)
```

This interpretation is somewhat arbitrary, but is part of the syntax of SNOBOL4. Parentheses can always be used for grouping terms in a desired way. Thus in the statement

```
        (X  Y)  Z
```

the subject is X concatenated with Y and the pattern is Z.

**Statements and Lines**

Programs are usually prepared on punched cards. In any event, programs are prepared line by line. If a statement has a label, that label must be first. If a statement starts on a new line, the label must therefore appear at the beginning of the line. On punched cards, this is column one.

Only the first 72 characters of a line may be used. If a statement is too long to fit on a line, it may be continued on successive lines, following certain rules about continuation. These rules are:

(a) A statement may be divided between lines at any point where a blank is mandatory or optional in the syntax of SNOBOL4. Examples are the blanks that separate statement components, the blanks that surround binary operators, and the blanks that indicate concatenation.

(b) A statement may *not* be divided in the middle of a data string, even if there are blanks in the data string. A blank in a data string has no syntactic significance and cannot be used as a dividing point.

(c) A line that is a continuation of a statement that started on a preceding line must begin with the symbol +.

(d) There is no limit to the number of continuation lines a statement may have.

More than one statement may appear on a line. A semicolon may be used to terminate a statement, and another statement may follow a semicolon. If a statement following a semicolon has a label, that label must begin immediately after the semicolon, without intervening blanks. An example is

```
        I   =   1  ;LOOP   I   =   LT(I,N) I + 1
```

The second statement on the line has the label LOOP.

There are many other aspects of the syntax of SNOBOL4 that are too involved to present here. A thorough comprehension of the syntax is not required for programming. Most commonly used constructions can be found in the examples given in the body of the book. These examples illustrate correct usage which can be imitated or referred to if questions arise.

APPENDIX B

# Summary of Functions and Operators

Listed below are the functions, predicates, and operators described in this book and the sections where they are described.

### Functions

| *Name* | *Operation Performed* | *Section* |
|---|---|---|
| ANY | pattern construction | 4.2 |
| ARRAY | array creation | 6.1 |
| BREAK | pattern construction | 4.2 |
| CONVERT | data type conversion | 6.2 |
| DATA | data type definition | 6.3 |
| DEFINE | function definition | 5.1 |
| DETACH | association removal | 7.4 |
| DUPL | string duplication | 3.5 |
| INPUT | input association | 7.1, 7.2, 7.3 |
| LEN | pattern construction | 2.7, 4.2 |
| NOTANY | pattern construction | 4.2 |
| OUTPUT | output association | 7.1, 7.2, 7.3 |
| POS | pattern construction | 4.2 |
| REMDR | numerical computation | 2.4, 3.2 |
| REPLACE | character replacement | 3.5 |
| REWIND | file positioning | 7.4 |
| RPOS | pattern construction | 4.2 |

| *Name* | *Operation Performed* | *Section* |
|---|---|---|
| RTAB | pattern construction | 4.2 |
| SIZE | string length | 2.4, 3.8 |
| SPAN | pattern construction | 4.2 |
| TAB | pattern construction | 4.2 |
| TABLE | table creation | 6.2 |
| TRACE | trace association | 9.2 |
| TRIM | string trimming | 3.5 |

**Predicates**

| *Name* | *Type of Comparison* | *Section* |
|---|---|---|
| DIFFER | object | 2.6 |
| EQ | numerical | 2.6, 3.1 |
| GE | numerical | 3.1 |
| GT | numerical | 3.1, 3.8 |
| IDENT | object | 2.6, 3.7, 3.8 |
| LE | numerical | 3.1 |
| LGT | string | 3.7 |
| LT | numerical | 2.6, 3.1 |
| NE | numerical | 3.1 |

**Binary Operators**

| *Symbol* | *Operation Performed* | *Associativity* | *Relative Precedence* | *Section* |
|---|---|---|---|---|
| $ | immediate assignment | left | 7 | 4.4, 4.5 |
| . | conditional assignment | left | 7 | 2.8, 4.5 |
| !, ** | exponentiation | right | 6 | 3.1 |
| * | multiplication | left | 5 | 2.3, 3.1 |
| / | division | left | 4 | 2.3, 3.1, 3.2 |
| + | addition | left | 3 | 2.3, 3.1 |
| - | subtraction | left | 3 | 2.3, 3.1 |
| blank | concatenation | left | 2 | 2.3, 2.7, 4.5 |
| | | alternation | left | 1 | 2.7, 4.5 |

**Unary Operators**

| *Symbol* | *Operation Performed* | *Section* |
|---|---|---|
| $ | indirect reference | 3.6 |
| * | unevaluated expression | 4.3 |
| + | positive | 3.1 |
| - | negative | 3.1 |
| & | keyword | see next section |

**Keywords**

| *Name* | *Initial Value* | *Section* |
|---|---|---|
| &ALPHABET | character set | 3.7 |
| &ANCHOR | 0 | 4.1 |
| &DUMP | 0 | 2.2, 9.3 |
| &FTRACE | 0 | 9.2 |
| &STCOUNT | 0 | 9.3 |
| &STFCOUNT | 0 | 9.3 |
| &STLIMIT | 50000 | 9.4 |
| &TRACE | 0 | 9.2 |
| &TRIM | 0 | 3.5 |

This book describes only the basic aspects of SNOBOL4. There are a number of more specialized functions, operations, and keywords as well as additional uses for those described in this book. For a complete description of the SNOBOL4 language, see Reference 1.

APPENDIX C

# Preparing and Running a SNOBOL4 Program

SNOBOL4 is available on many different types of computers in a variety of environments. The details of preparing and running a SNOBOL4 program may vary from one location to another. The major factors that may differ are:

(a) The type of computer available.

(b) The nature of the operating system that supervises the running of programs.

(c) The type of input and output devices used for preparing the program and obtaining the results.

(d) Local conventions and rules for referring to data files.

(e) The particular implementation of SNOBOL4 that is available.

The situation usually is not as bad as the factors above might imply. There are a few major differences and some minor considerations, but, on the whole, SNOBOL4 programs may be run in nearly the same way at most locations.

The original implementation of SNOBOL4 developed at Bell Laboratories (see References 1 and 4) is available for most large-scale scientific computers including the IBM 360/370, CDC 6000 series, UNIVAC 1108, Sigma 5/6/7, DEC System-10, RCA Spectra 70, and GE635. This implementation is largely independent of the type of computer on which it is installed, except for differences in character sets. Some implementations handle data files differently, and some implementations have a few extra features. SNOBOL4 described in this book corresponds to Version 3 of the Bell Laboratories implementation.

Earlier versions lack some features of Version 3. Refer to local documentation for the particular version you are using.

There are a few other implementations of SNOBOL4 that are distinctly different. An implementation called SPITBOL is most notable (see Reference 5). This implementation contains a number of extra features and differs somewhat from other implementations. Again, users should refer to documentation at their location. There are also SNOBOL languages other than SNOBOL4. Some, such as SNOBOL3, are precursors of SNOBOL4. Others are offshoots which may resemble SNOBOL4 to some extent, but differ markedly in actual language features. If a SNOBOL translator is not specifically identified with SNOBOL4, an investigation should be undertaken before attempting to use it.

The operating system depends on the type of computer available, and there are several different operating systems for some computers. The most noticeable difference to the programmer is whether the operating system supports time-shared, interactive use from a computer terminal. SNOBOL4 was originally developed for "batch" use in which a program is submitted as a deck of cards, and the results are returned as printed output. A number of operating systems support SNOBOL4 in an interactive environment, where a program may be entered from a Teletype ® or other computer terminal, or stored on a data file for future correction and use. Interactive systems vary considerably, and programmers who plan to use SNOBOL4 in such an environment should first familiarize themselves with the general use of interactive computing.

Most commonly, SNOBOL4 programs are submitted in a batch mode as a deck of cards. Such a deck usually has the following structure:

control cards
SNOBOL4 program
data to be read

Control cards typically serve to identify the user, to establish the names of data files, and to indicate that a SNOBOL4 program is to be run. Control cards depend on the particular operating system and on local conventions. Usually a few cards are sufficient for running most SNOBOL4 programs. Once these cards have been determined, they usually need be of little further concern. Data to be read by the SNOBOL4 program follows the END card which terminates the program.

Many programmers learning SNOBOL4 will already know how to use their local computer center and its equipment. Even for the complete novice, only a small investment in instruction and practice will be sufficient to write simple programs. Additional knowledge can be acquired as more complicated programs are attempted.

APPENDIX D

# Solutions to Exercises

*Solution 2.1*

| *integers* | *data strings* | *names* | *labels* |
|---|---|---|---|
| 0 | 'S' | COUNT | READ |
| 1 | 'THE TOTAL COUNT IS ' | OUTPUT | AGAIN |
| | | INPUT | EOF |
| | | TEXT | END |

*Solution 2.2*

```
I   =   100

J   =   10000

K   =   13

L   =   1308

WORD1   =   'COGITO'

WORD2   =   'ERGO'

WORD3   =   'SUM'

CLAUSE   =   'COGITO ERGO SUM'
```

```
SENTENCE   =   'COGITO ERGO SUM.'

ENDVOWEL   =   PATTERN

V   =   'O'
```

The pattern ENDVOWEL matches any vowel that is followed by a blank. The value assigned to V results from the pattern-matching statement using ENDVOWEL.

*Solution 2.3*

```
DIGIT   =   '0' | '2' | '4' | '6' | '8'

PUNC   =   ',' | '.' | ':' | '!' | ';'

VWLP   =   VOWEL PUNC

DVWL3   =   VOWEL LEN(3) VOWEL
```

VOWEL is the pattern given in Section 2.7.

*Solution 2.4*

One way to solve this problem is to reverse the string as described in Program 4 of Section 2.11. Then the statement

```
IDENT(STRING,REVERSE)                              :S(YES)F(NO)
```

performs the desired test. To avoid destroying the value of STRING when forming REVERSE, first execute

```
TEXT   =   STRING
```

and then proceed as described in Section 2.11.

*Solution 2.5*

```
STRING   LEN(N) . H   =                            :F(CANT)

STRING   =   STRING H
```

The failure goto CANT assumes that a string of less than N characters is not to be rotated.

*Solution 2.6*

```
READ   OUTPUT   =   INPUT                          :F(END)

       PUNCH   =   OUTPUT                          :(READ)

END
```

*Solution 3.1*

| *parenthesized expression* | *value* |
|---|---|
| `(3 / 2) + (5 * 6)` | `31` |
| `3 / (2 * 6)` | `0` |
| `(3 * 2) / 6` | `1` |
| `(2.0 + (0 / 3)) - 6.7` | `-4.7` |
| `('7' * '3.5') / REMDR(5,7)` | `4.9` |
| `(SIZE(DUPL('**',3)) * 2.0) + REMDR(31,100)` | `43.0` |
| `3 (5 + 21)` | `'326'` |
| `REMDR(37,15) (REMDR(15,37) * 2)` | `'730'` |

The quotation marks surrounding the last two values indicate data strings resulting from concatenation.

*Solution 3.2*

```
        &TRIM   =   1
        COUNT   =   0
        SUM   =   0.0
READ    OUTPUT   =   INPUT                         :F(RESULT)
        SUMS   =   SUM + OUTPUT
        COUNT   =   COUNT + 1                      :(READ)
RESULT  OUTPUT   =   'AVERAGE IS ' SUM / COUNT
END
```

*Solution 3.3*

```
        &TRIM   =   1
        N   =   INPUT                              :F(ERROR)
        M   =   INPUT                              :F(ERROR)
        I   =   0
```

```
LOOP    I   =     LT(I,M) I + 1                              :F(END)
        OUTPUT    =   DUPL('.',N)                            :(LOOP)
ERROR   OUTPUT    =   '*** MISSING DATA ***'
END
```

*Solution 3.4*

```
        I   =     1
NEXTL   J   =     I * I
        COL1     =   DUPL(' ',10 - SIZE(I)) I
        COL2     =   DUPL(' ',10 - SIZE(J)) J
        OUTPUT    =   COL1 COL2
        I   =     LT(I,25) I + 1                             :S(NEXTL)
END
```

The two columns could be constructed in the statement that performs the output. Three separate statements are used for clarity.

*Solution 3.5*

```
        ALPHA   =   'ABCDEFGHIJKLMNOPQRSTUVWXYZ'
        REVAL   =   'ZYXWVUTSRQPONMLKJIHGFEDCBA'
ENCODE  LINE    =   INPUT                                    :F(END)
        OUTPUT   =   REPLACE(LINE,ALPHA,REVAL)               :(ENCODE)
END
```

*Solution 3.6*

The value of $NOUN and $$NOUN are both NOUN as may be seen from the following diagram.

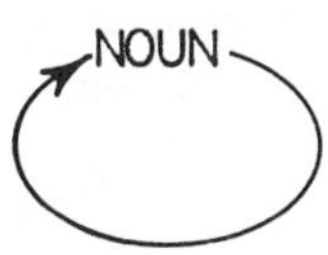

*Solution 3.7*

```
        &TRIM   =   1
READ    WORD    =   INPUT                    :F(DONE)
        $WORD   =   SIZE(WORD)               :(READ)
```

The value assigned to HAT is 3, to CLAPTRAP is 8, and to PERSIMMON is 9.

*Solution 4.1*

The first time DEL is executed, neither E nor I match the L at cursor position zero. The cursor is advanced, and E matches at cursor position 1. This character is deleted by replacement with the null string. The second time DEL is executed, the process is repeated. Each alternative is matched at each successive cursor position until a match for E is found at cursor position 5. Again the E is deleted. On the third execution, E is again found in cursor position 5, and is deleted. On the fourth execution there is no match until the cursor is advanced to position 6. Here the second alternative, I, is matched and deleted. The pattern match succeeds twice more, then fails when there are no more Es or Is in the value of TEXT. The successive values of TEXT are:

```
LET SLEEPING DOGS LIE
LT SLEEPING DOGS LIE
LT SLEPING DOGS LIE
LT SLPING DOGS LIE
LT SLPNG DOGS LIE
LT SLPNG DOGS LE
LT SLPNG DOGS L
```

*Solution 4.2*

P1: Any string containing two vowels.
P2: Any string containing two non-consecutive vowels.
P3: Any string containing a vowel in the first five characters and a vowel as the sixth character.
P4: Any string containing vowels as the seventh and eighth characters.
P5: Any string containing a vowel among its last three characters.
P6: Any string containing a digit.
P7: Any string beginning with a digit.

P8: Any string that does not begin with an asterisk.
P9: Any string containing a consecutive group of one or more digits, followed by a period.
P10: Any string containing a balanced substring enclosed within parentheses.
P11: Any string that is balanced and enclosed in parentheses.
P12: Any string containing two occurrences of the same vowel.
P13: Any string in which there are N consecutive blanks, starting at the tenth character.

*Solution 4.3*

```
PA   =   RTAB(1) NOTANY('*')

PB   =   BREAK('AEIOU') LEN(1) BREAK('AEIOU')

PC   =   LEN(11)

PD   =   POS(0) SPAN('AEIOU') RPOS(0)

PE   =   LEN(1) $ CH BREAK(*CH) LEN(1) BREAK(*CH)
```

*Solution 4.4*

```
        LETTER   =   'ABCDEFGHIJKLMNOPQRSTUVWXYZ'

        WPAT   =   BREAK(LETTER) SPAN(LETTER)

        COUNT   =   0

READ    LINE   =   INPUT                              :F(RESULT)

NEXTW   LINE   WPAT   =                               :F(READ)

        COUNT   =   COUNT + 1                         :(NEXTW)

RESULT  OUTPUT   =   'THERE ARE ' COUNT ' WORDS'

END
```

*Solution 4.5*

The definition of a word is more complicated than it appears at first glance. There are compound words, containing hyphens, for example. Forms that include apostrophes, such as possessives and contractions, present another problem. Numerals are sometimes considered to be words. Technical material presents a variety of problems. The following sentence, although contrived, illustrates some of the problems.

```
NEARLY 1/2 OF ALL MULTI-TRACK TAPES ARE USED IN AN I/O

ENVIRONMENT WHICH ISN'T INCLUDED IN THE D+N/L RELATION.
```

For this sentence, WPAT matches, among other things, the "nonwords" MULTI, I, O, ISN, T, D, N, and L.

*Solution 5.1*

```
          DEFINE('MATRIX(C,N,M)I')
                      .
                      .
                      .
                      .
MATRIX    I     =     0
MATPRT    I     =     LT(I,M) I + 1                    :F(RETURN)
          OUTPUT   =     DUPL(C,N)                     :(MATPRT)
```

*Solution 5.2*

```
          DEFINE('DELETE(S,C)')
                      .
                      .
                      .
DELETE    S   SPAN(C)     =                            :S(DELETE)
          DELETE   =     S                             :(RETURN)
```

*Solution 5.3*

```
          DEFINE('SUBSTR(S,N,M)')
                      .
                      .
                      .
SUBSTR    S   TAB(N - 1) LEN(M) . SUBSTR               :S(RETURN)F(FRETURN)
```

*Solution 5.4*

```
         DEFINE('PALIN(S)')
                  .
                  .
                  .
PALIN    IDENT(S,REVERSE(S))                    :S(RETURN)F(FRETURN)
```

This solution uses the function REVERSE developed in Section 5.1.

*Solution 5.5*

Change the procedure for PALIN to:

```
PALIN    S   =   DELETE(S,' ')
         IDENT(S,REVERSE(S))                    :S(RETURN)F(FRETURN)
```

*Solution 5.6*

```
         DEFINE('F(N)')
                  .
                  .
                  .
F        F   =   EQ(N,0) 0                      :S(RETURN)
         F   =   EQ(N,1) 1                      :S(RETURN)
         F   =   F(N - 1) + F(N - 2)            :(RETURN)
```

The Fibonacci numbers provide a sequence of integers which are interesting because of their relationship to population growth and proportions and symmetries found in nature. For more information, see References 6 and 7. It is not necessary to know anything about Fibonacci numbers to solve this exercise, however. All the necessary information is contained in the recursive definition. It is necessary to realize that

$$f(n+1) = f(n)+f(n-1) \qquad n > 1$$

is equivalent to

$$f(n)=f(n-1)+f(n-2) \qquad n>2$$

The value of F(6) is 8.

*Solution 5.7*

```
          DEFINE('POST(EXP)L,R,OP')
          PREPAT    =  POS(0) LEN(1) . OP '(' BAL . L ','
+                      BAL . R ')'
                       .
                       .
                       .
POST      POST  =    EXP
          POST  PREPAT  =    '(' POST(L) ',' POST(R) ')' OP
+                                                     :(RETURN)
```

*Solution 6.1*

If a word longer than ten characters is encountered, the reference to the array LENGTH fails. Since the goto is unconditional, such a word is simply ignored. The array could be made larger, of course. At some point, however, the likelihood of a word that is too long becomes very small. A warning message could be provided as follows:

```
          LENGTH<N>    =    LENGTH<N>  + 1              :S(NEXTW)
          OUTPUT    =     '*** LONG WORD ***'           :(NEXTW)
```

There are a variety of increasingly sophisticated ways of handling this problem.

*Solution 6.2*

```
          POWERS    =    ARRAY('10,5')
          I    =    1
ASSIGN    POWERS<I,1>    =    I
          POWERS<I,2>    =    I ! 2
          POWERS<I,3>    =    I ! 3
          POWERS<I,4>    =    I ! 4
          POWERS<I,5>    =    I ! 5
          I    =    LT(I,10) I + 1                      :S(ASSIGN)
```

*Solution 6.3*

```
          CHAR    =   LEN(1) . C
          CCOUNT  =   TABLE()
READ      LINE    =   INPUT                                    :F(RESULT)
          OUTPUT  =   LINE
NEXTC     LINE  CHAR  =                                        :F(READ)
          CCOUNT<C>  =  CCOUNT<C> + 1                          :(NEXTC)
RESULT    ALPHA   =   &ALPHABET
          OUTPUT  =
          OUTPUT  =   'THE CHARACTER COUNTS ARE:'
NEXTA     ALPHA  CHAR  =                                       :F(END)
          OUTPUT  =   C '  ' CCOUNT<C>                         :(NEXTA)
END
```

This solution simply prints the result for every possible character. Since the characters that may be referenced in the table are available in &ALPHABET, it is not necessary to convert the table CCOUNT to an array.

*Solution 6.4*

The word-counting program given in Section 6.2 can be modified easily to count only four-letter words. Simply insert the following statement after NEXTW.

```
          EQ(SIZE(WORD),4)                                     :F(NEXTW)
```

*Solution 6.5*

```
          DATA('COMPLEX(R,I)')
```

R represents the real part of a complex number and I the imaginary part.

*Solution 6.6*

```
        DEFINE('ADD(C1,C2)')
        DEFINE('SUB(C1,C2)')
        DEFINE('MPY(C1,C2)')
        DEFINE('DIV(C1,C2)SQ')
                        .
                        .
                        .
ADD     ADD  =  COMPLEX(R(C1) + R(C2),I(C1) + I(C2))
+                                                  :(RETURN)
SUB     SUB  =  COMPLEX(R(C1) - R(C2),I(C1) - I(C2))
+                                                  :(RETURN)
MPY     MPY  =  COMPLEX(R(C1) * R(C2) - I(C1) * I(C2),
+                R(C1) * I(C2) + I(C1) * R(C2))    :(RETURN)
DIV     SQ   =  R(C2) * R(C2) + I(C2) * I(C2)
        DIV  =  COMPLEX((R(C1) * R(C2) + I(C1) * I(C2))
+               / SQ,(I(C1) * R(C2) - R(C1) * I(C2)) / SQ)
+                                                  :(RETURN)
```

See Solution 6.5 for the definition of COMPLEX.

*Solution 6.7*

```
        DEFINE('IDSUBJ(S1,S2)')
                        .
                        .
                        .
IDSUBJ IDENT(SUBJ(S1),SUBJ(S2))                    :S(RETURN)F(FRETURN)
```

*Solution 6.8*

```
          DEFINE('XSONS(NODE)T')
                    .
                    .
                    .
XSONS     T   =   LSON(NODE)
          LSON(NODE)   =   RSON(NODE)
          RSON(NODE)   =   T                          :(RETURN)
```

*Solution 7.1*

```
          INPUT('IN',10,200)
          OUTPUT('OUT',20,'(200A1)')
COPY      OUT   =   IN                                :S(COPY)
END
```

*Solution 7.2*

```
          OUTPUT('VERT',6,'(1H ,1A1)')
DISP      VERT   =   INPUT                            :S(DISP)
END
```

By specifying one-character output lines, each character is forced onto a separate line.

*Solution 7.3*

```
          OUTPUT('ATTENTION',6,'(6H *****,127A1)')
```

*Solution 7.4*

```
          DEFINE('ARYPRT(A)I')
                    .
                    .
                    .
```

```
ARYPRT I    =    1

ARYNXT OUTPUT    =    A<I>                          :F(RETURN)

       I    =    I + 1                              :(ARYNXT)
```

*Solution 8.1*

The generation of an index concordance is very similar to counting words. Using a function CITE for noting that a word occurs on a line, the following basic program may be used.

```
NEXTW   WORD   =   GETW()                           :F(DONE)

        CITE(INDEX,WORD)                            :(NEXTW)

DONE    PRINT(INDEX)

END
```

The procedure for GETW developed in Section 8.1 needs minor modifications to keep track of line numbers. PRINT can be used without modification. A complete program follows.

```
        LINE.NO    =    0

        LETTER    =    'ABCDEFGHIJKLMNOPQRSTUVWXYZ'

        WPAT    =    BREAK(LETTER) SPAN(LETTER) . GETW

        INDEX    =    TABLE()

        DEFINE('GETW()')

        DEFINE('CITE(TABLE,STRING)')

        DEFINE('PRINT(TABLE)ARRAY,I')

NEXTW   WORD    =    GETW()                         :F(DONE)

        CITE(INDEX,WORD)                            :(NEXTW)

DONE    PRINT(INDEX)                                :(END)

GETW    LINE    WPAT    =                           :S(RETURN)

        LINE    =    INPUT                          :F(FRETURN)

        LINE.NO    =    LINE.NO + 1

        OUTPUT    =    LINE '  ' LINE.NO            :(GETW)
```

```
CITE    TABLE<STRING>  =   TABLE<STRING> LINE.NO  ', '
+                                                   :(RETURN)
PRINT   OUTPUT   =
        ARRAY   =   CONVERT(TABLE,'ARRAY')          :F(NONE)
        I   =   1
RESULT  OUTPUT   =   ARRAY<I,1> ' - ' ARRAY<I,2>    :F(RETURN)
        I   =   I + 1                               :(RESULT)
NONE    OUTPUT   =   'THERE ARE NONE'               :(RETURN)
END
```

*Solution 8.2*

```
        DEFINE('LPAD(S,N)')
        DEFINE('RPAD(S,N)')
              .
              .
              .
LPAD    LPAD   =  DUPL(' ',N - SIZE(S)) S           :(RETURN)
RPAD    RPAD   =  S DUPL(' ',N - SIZE(S))           :(RETURN)
```

Exercise 3.4 only requires the use of LPAD. The desired output is created by the following statements:

```
        I   =   1
NEXTR   OUTPUT   =   LPAD(I,10) LPAD(I * I,10)
        I   =   LT(I,25) I + 1                      :S(NEXTR)F(END)
```

*Solution 8.3*

```
        DEFINE('GETW(WLIST,N)I')
        WLPAT   =   BREAK(',') . GETW LEN(1)
                    .
                    .
                    .
GETW    I  =    1
GETW    WLIST   WLPAT  =                            :F(FRETURN)
        I   =   LT(I,N) I + 1                       :S(GETWN)F(RETURN)
```

This function fails if WLIST does not contain N words. If N is less than 1, the first word is returned. GETW requires the execution of about 2N statements. The array representation is accessed with only one statement, regardless of the value of N.

*Solution 8.4*

```
        DEFINE('GETC(WCOUNT,WORD)T,I')
                    .
                    .
                    .
GETC    I   =   1
GETCN   T   =   WCOUNT<I,1>                         :F(FRETURN)
        GETC   =   IDENT(T,WORD) WCOUNT<I,2>        :S(RETURN)
        I   =   I + 1                               :(GETCN)
```

This function fails if WORD is not in WCOUNT. GETC requires the execution of about 3 statements for every word that must be examined in the array. The number of words that have to be examined depends on their order in the array. On the average, the number of words that have to be examined might be expected to be N/2. The table representation is accessed with only one statement, regardless of the value of WORD.

*Solution 8.5*

(a) The most convenient data format, from a programming point of view, would place one word, left-justified, in each data record. Statements to construct an array of words follow.

```
        &TRIM   =   1
        WLIST   =   ARRAY('100')
        I   =   1
READW   WORD   =   INPUT                              :F(DONE)
        WLIST<I>   =   WORD                           :F(OVER)
        I   =   I + 1                                 :(READW)
```

(b) To minimize the number of data records required, the words could be written as one long string, separated by commas. When the end of one record is reached, the next record is started without interruption. Thus words may be divided between records. Statements to construct an array of words based on this data format follow.

```
        &TRIM   =   1
        NEXTW   =   BREAK(',') . WORD LEN(1)
        WLIST   =   ARRAY('100')
        I   =   1
READ    LINE   =   INPUT                              :F(DONE)
GETW    LINE   NEXTW   =                              :F(READ)
        WLIST<I>   =   WORD                           :F(OVER)
        I   =   I + 1                                 :(GETW)
```

Format (a) is easy to prepare, proofread, and correct, but requires many records that may contain much unused space. Of course this format assumes there are no words longer than the length of a record. Format (b) is concise, but is difficult to prepare, proofread, and correct. Corrections are especially difficult if a change in length is necessary, since that affects all subsequent records. Notice, however, that the program used for this format will accept records with trailing blanks as if they are simply shorter. Thus, a compromise data format might allow shorter records resulting from deletions or insertions.

*Solution 8.6*

The following program converts from format (a) to format (b):

```
        &TRIM   =   1

BUILD   WLIST   =   WLIST INPUT ','                    :S(BUILD)

        PUNCH   =   WLIST

END
```

The following program converts from format (b) to format (a):

```
        &TRIM   =   1

        GETW    =   BREAK(',') . PUNCH LINE(1)

READ    LINE    =   LINE INPUT                         :F(END)

NEXTW   LINE    GETW   =                               :S(NEXTW)F(READ)

END
```

*Solution 8.7*

Since a string may contain any character, no character can be used as a separator. In many practical cases, at least one character may be known not to occur in the particular strings to be used, and hence this character can be used as a separator. In the most general case, however, this way of representing a list of strings cannot be used. One way to represent a list of strings as a string is to use a technique similar to the Hollerith literals described in Section 7.3. In such a representation, the character count permits the determination of the substring without regard for the particular characters in it. Thus, Hollerith literals can be written in succession to represent a string of strings. An example is

```
6H      4H,,,,1HH
```

which represents a string of six blanks, a string of four commas, and a single H.

*Solution 8.8*

To determine the best way of representing data, more detailed specifications than those given in Exercise 8.8 are necessary. However, general remarks can be made.

(a) A checkerboard is naturally represented as a two-dimensional, 8-by-8 array where each square is designated by its numerical coordinates. See Figure D.1.

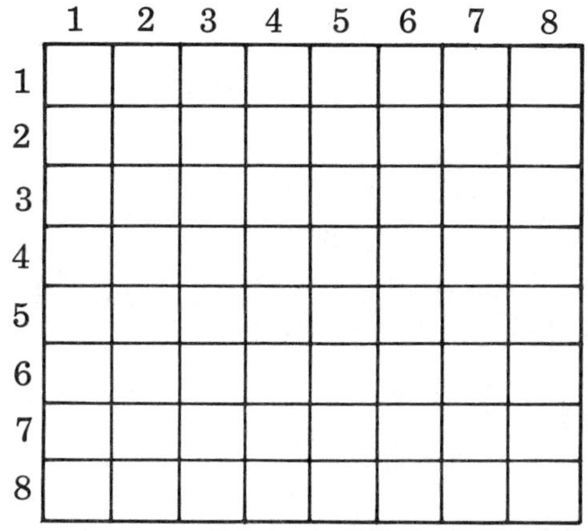

**Figure D.1** A Checkerboard

If the board is created by the statement

```
BOARD   =   ARRAY('8,8')
```

then the upper left square is referenced by `BOARD<1,1>`, and so on.

(b) An address list is a sequence of entries. Each entry may be more than one line. While it is logical to think of an address list as an array of strings, most address lists are too large to be kept in memory intact. A data file is a better solution. Printing an address list only involves reading and printing the file. Updating an address list—making corrections, insertions, and deletions—is more complicated. The simplest process is to read the address list file, make corrections in sequence, and write a new, updated file. A program which updates a file is called an editor.

(c) Objects in an archaeological collection typically have certain common attributes. Examples are identification number, date, site, material, and so on. For many purposes, such objects are best represented by a programmer-defined data type which represents the attributes of interest as fields. For more information on this subject, see References 8 and 9.

(d) A table of contents for a book is usually represented as a sequence of lines. There is more structure in a table of contents than simply its sequence, however. Usually a table of contents has subheadings, indicated by indentation. There may be several levels of indentation. An example, taken from Reference 1, is:

.

.

.

Chapter 2—Pattern Matching

2.1 Introduction

2.2 Alternation and Concatenation

2.3 Scanning

2.4 Modes of Scanning

2.4.1 Unanchored Mode

2.4.2 Anchored Mode

.

.

.

This structure is basically hierarchical and can be represented by a tree as illustrated in Figure D.2.

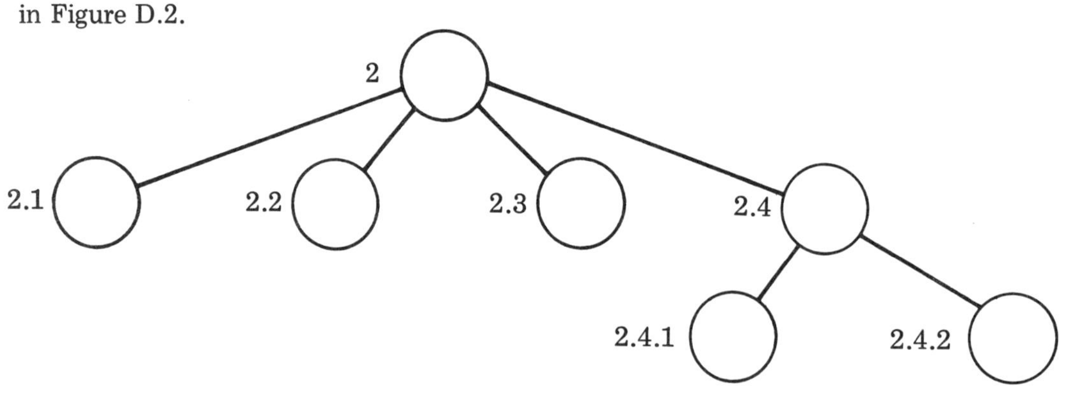


**Figure D.2** A Table of Contents Tree

The nodes in the tree might contain the actual text of the headings. This type of tree is more general than the binary tree since a node may have more than two sons. For a detailed discussion of trees and related structures, see Reference 12.

(e) A musical score is an extremely complicated structure. In order to transform a score into data that can be read into a program, it is necessary to represent a two-dimensional structure in which a large variety of symbols with various meanings may occur. In addition, there are general characteristics, such as tempo and key, which apply to sections of the score, but may change from section to section. To locate specific configurations or search for repeated themes, pattern matching might be used. In this case, a string representation might be the best internal format. For representing all the interrelationships of the parts of a musical score, a more complicated structure might be more useful. Many attempts have been made to develop adequate representations for musical scores. These attempts have only been partially successful so far. For further reading, see References 10 and 11.

*Solution 9.1*

The first statement has too many parentheses and the last has too few. The second statement contains an odd number of quotation marks. The subject of the third statement is not a legal name. Corresponding corrected statements follow.

```
        EQ(SIZE(S),N)                                      :S(OKAY)

        OUTPUT   =   'THE RESULT IS ' S ' AT TERMINATION'

        A1   =   INPUT

        N   =   LT(N,SIZE(M)) N + 1                        :F(DONE)
```

*Solution 9.2*

To limit execution and obtain a string dump, the following statements might occur at the beginning of the program:

```
        &STLIMIT   =   1000

        &DUMP   =   1
```

In addition, tracing might be obtained by the statements

```
        &TRACE   =   1000

        &FTRACE   =   1000
```

and appropriate trace associations.

*Solution 9.3*

A program to count the number of different words on a data file is:

```
        &TRACE   =   1000                                          1
        TRACE('COUNT')                                             2
        TRACE('WORD')                                              3
        LETTER   =   'ABCDEFGHIJKLMNOPQRSTUVWXYZ'                  4
        WPAT   =   BREAK(LETTER) SPAN(LETTER) . WORD               5
        DIFF   =   TABLE()                                         6
        COUNT   =   0                                              7
READ    LINE   =   INPUT                          :F(RESULT)       8
NEXTW   LINE   WPAT   =                           :F(READ)         9
        DIFF<WORD>   =   IDENT(DIFF<WORD>) 1      :F(NEXTW)        10
        COUNT   =   COUNT + 1                     :(NEXTW)         11
RESULT  OUTPUT   =   'THERE ARE ' COUNT ' DIFFERENT WORDS'         12
END                                                                13
```

When a new word is encountered, it is "marked" by assigning it the value 1 in the table DIFF. If the word is encountered later, it is found to have a nonnull value in DIFF, and is not counted. A typical section of output produced by this program follows.

```
STATEMENT 7: COUNT = 0,TIME = 7
STATEMENT 9: WORD = 'YOU',TIME = 14
STATEMENT 11: COUNT = 1,TIME = 19
STATEMENT 9: WORD = 'CAN',TIME = 24
STATEMENT 11: COUNT = 2,TIME = 30
STATEMENT 9: WORD = 'FOOL',TIME = 36
STATEMENT 11: COUNT = 3,TIME = 41
STATEMENT 9: WORD = 'SOME',TIME = 46
```

```
STATEMENT 11: COUNT = 4,TIME = 51

STATEMENT 9: WORD = 'OF',TIME = 57

STATEMENT 11: COUNT = 5,TIME = 62

STATEMENT 9: WORD = 'THE',TIME = 68

STATEMENT 11: COUNT = 6,TIME = 74

STATEMENT 9: WORD = 'PEOPLE',TIME = 79

STATEMENT 11: COUNT = 7,TIME = 84

STATEMENT 9: WORD = 'ALL',TIME = 90

STATEMENT 11: COUNT = 8,TIME = 95

STATEMENT 9: WORD = 'OF',TIME = 101

STATEMENT 9: WORD = 'THE',TIME = 108

STATEMENT 9: WORD = 'TIME',TIME = 117

STATEMENT 11: COUNT = 9,TIME = 122

STATEMENT 9: WORD = 'AND',TIME = 130

STATEMENT 11: COUNT = 10,TIME = 136

                •

                •

                •
```

*Solution 9.4*

A complete program for tracing the computation of F(5) follows.

```
&FTRACE    =    1000

DEFINE('F(N)')

OUTPUT    =    'F(5)=' F(5)                    :(END)
```

```
F      F  =  EQ(N,0) 0                        :S(RETURN)      4
       F  =  EQ(N,1) 1                        :S(RETURN)      5
       F  =  F(N - 1) + F(N - 2)              :(RETURN)       6
END                                                           7
```

The output produced by this program is:

```
STATEMENT 3: LEVEL 0 CALL OF F(5),TIME = 5
STATEMENT 6: LEVEL 1 CALL OF F(4),TIME = 10
STATEMENT 6: LEVEL 2 CALL OF F(3),TIME = 15
STATEMENT 6: LEVEL 3 CALL OF F(2),TIME = 21
STATEMENT 6: LEVEL 4 CALL OF F(1),TIME = 26
STATEMENT 5: LEVEL 4 RETURN OF F = 1,TIME = 30
STATEMENT 6: LEVEL 4 CALL OF F(0),TIME = 34
STATEMENT 4: LEVEL 4 RETURN OF F = 0,TIME = 37
STATEMENT 6: LEVEL 3 RETURN OF F = 1,TIME = 40
STATEMENT 6: LEVEL 3 CALL OF F(1),TIME = 44
STATEMENT 5: LEVEL 3 RETURN OF F = 1,TIME = 48
STATEMENT 6: LEVEL 2 RETURN OF F = 2,TIME = 51
STATEMENT 6: LEVEL 2 CALL OF F(2),TIME = 55
STATEMENT 6: LEVEL 3 CALL OF F(1),TIME = 61
STATEMENT 5: LEVEL 3 RETURN OF F = 1,TIME = 65
STATEMENT 6: LEVEL 3 CALL OF F(0),TIME = 69
STATEMENT 4: LEVEL 3 RETURN OF F = 0,TIME = 72
STATEMENT 6: LEVEL 2 RETURN OF F = 1,TIME = 75
STATEMENT 6: LEVEL 1 RETURN OF F = 3,TIME = 78
```

```
STATEMENT 6: LEVEL 1 CALL OF F(3),TIME = 82

STATEMENT 6: LEVEL 2 CALL OF F(2),TIME = 87

STATEMENT 6: LEVEL 3 CALL OF F(1),TIME = 93

STATEMENT 5: LEVEL 3 RETURN OF F = 1,TIME = 96

STATEMENT 6: LEVEL 3 CALL OF F(0),TIME = 100

STATEMENT 4: LEVEL 3 RETURN OF F = 0,TIME = 105

STATEMENT 6: LEVEL 2 RETURN OF F = 1,TIME = 108

STATEMENT 6: LEVEL 2 CALL OF F(1),TIME = 112

STATEMENT 5: LEVEL 2 RETURN OF F = 1,TIME = 116

STATEMENT 6: LEVEL 1 RETURN OF F = 2,TIME = 119

STATEMENT 6: LEVEL 0 RETURN OF F = 5,TIME = 121

F(5)=5
```

This printout shows that the same value is computed a number of times, as required by intermediate computations. The example illustrates the wastefulness of recursive solutions in certain cases.

*Solution 9.5*

Assume an average word length of five characters. Allowing two characters per word for punctuation and trailing blanks on records, perhaps eleven words might be expected on each record. For each record, two statements are required for input and output and two are required for each word. Therefore an estimated 24 statements would be required to process each card, or 240 in all. For each different word, two statements are required for printing the results. Estimation of the number of different words is more difficult. The safest assumption is that every word is different. Some words, such as the articles A and THE, are likely to occur several times, however. To make a guess, perhaps 80 of the 110 expected words may be different. Thus 160 statements may be required to print the results. There are eight statements in the program that are executed just once, regardless of the number of words. This number is small compared to the total of 400 statements estimated for processing, and can be ignored. If this estimate is doubled, a reasonable value to assign to &STLIMIT would be 800. An actual run on data selected at random required 442 statements.

*Solution 9.6*

The function PRE itself works properly. The error in the program is the failure to trim blanks from input records. If an expression on a data record ends in a parenthesis, INP fails to match. Other malfunctions occur in other cases.

# Glossary

The definitions that are given in this glossary apply to the meaning of terms in the specialized contexts of computer programming, programming languages, and SNOBOL4 in particular.

**Algorithm.** A completely and precisely defined procedure for performing an operation.

**Alternation.** A binary operation that constructs a pattern in which the second operand is an alternative of the first operand.

**Alternative.** One of a number of pattern components, any of which may be matched. See **alternation.**

**Anchored mode.** The mode of pattern matching in which a substring that is matched must begin with the first character of the subject string. See **unanchored mode.**

**Argument.** A value supplied to a function and which is used by the function in its computation.

**Array.** A collection of variables referenced by integer subscripts. See **table.**

**Assignment.** The process of associating a value with a variable.

**Associativity.** The property of a binary operator that determines whether it groups to the left or to the right.

**Attached name.** A variable attached to a component of a pattern. See **conditional assignment** and **immediate assignment.**

**Balanced expression.** A string in which parentheses are properly paired, as in an arithmetic expression.

**Binary operator.** An operator that has two operands.

**Buffer.** An area in memory where data being read in or written out is kept.

**Bug.** An error in a program.

**Built-in function.** A function that is part of the SNOBOL4 system.

**Built-in pattern.** A pattern that is part of the SNOBOL4 system and is the initial value of a name.

**Carriage control.** The first character of a string to be printed, used to control the printing mechanism.

**Character.** Any single symbol.

**Character set.** The collection of all the characters available on a particular computer.

**Character-set pattern.** A pattern in which matching is determined by a set of characters, but not by the order in which they appear.

**Compilation.** The process of converting a program into an internal form which is suitable for computer execution.

**Computed goto.** A goto in which the label to which control is to be transferred is determined by a computation.

**Concatenation.** A binary operation that appends one string to another or that constructs a pattern in which the second operand is a subsequent of the first operand.

**Conditional assignment.** Assignment to an attached name which is conditional on the successful match of the entire pattern. See **immediate assignment.**

**Conditional goto.** A goto which transfers control conditionally, depending on the success or failure of the statement in which the goto appears. See **unconditional goto.**

**Conditional operation.** An operation whose successful completion depends on the existence of a specified situation. See **success** and **failure.**

**Continuation.** A method of preparing statements using more than one line.

**CPU.** The central processing unit of a computer in which instructions are executed.

**Cursor.** The character position in a string on which pattern matching is being performed.

**Data representation.** The way that data is formatted in terms of the structures available in a programming language.

**Data string.** A string used as data in a program.

**Data type.** The classification of data which divides data into categories depending on its properties.

**Debugging.** The process of locating and correcting program errors.

**Defined data object.** An instance of defined data type.

**Defined data type.** A data type that is introduced during program execution by use of the DATA function.

**Defined function.** A function that is introduced during program execution by use of the DEFINE function. See **procedure**.

**Diagnostics.** Information that assists in locating troubles in a program.

**End of file.** A condition that occurs when the end of a data file is reached.

**End statement.** The last statement in a SNOBOL4 program, identified by the label END .

**Error condition.** The result of an erroneous operation in a program.

**Execution.** The process of performing the operations specified in a program.

**Expression.** A basic component of a program which has a value when executed. Functions, operations, and references are typical expressions.

**Failure.** A condition that occurs when an operation cannot be performed or a specified relationship does not exist. See **success**.

**Field function.** A variable that references a field of a defined data object.

**File.** A sequence of records.

**File number.** An integer used to identify a particular file.

**Formal argument.** A name in a defined function that is used to pass the value of an argument to the procedure for the function.

**Format.** A specification used to describe the way a string is to be output.

**Function.** An operation that is identified by a name and operates on values given as arguments.

**Function call.** The execution of a function.

**Functional composition.** Use of previously developed functions in writing procedures for new functions.

**Global variable.** A variable whose value is not saved when a defined function is called and, hence, whose value can be changed by a function call.

**Goto.** A construction that specifies transfer of control to a labeled statement. See **label**.

**Identifier.** A string of characters, satisfying certain constraints, that is used to identify an object.

**Immediate assignment.** Assignment to an attached name which occurs when the component is matched, regardless of the success or failure of the entire pattern match. See **conditional assignment.**

**Indirect reference.** The use of a data string as a name.

**Infix notation.** A method of writing operations in which binary operators appear between their operands.

**Initial value.** The value given to a variable when it is created or used for the first time.

**Input.** The process of reading data into a program.

**Input association.** A relationship between a variable and a data file which causes a record to be read and assigned to the variable whenever the value of the variable is referenced.

**Instruction set.** The collection of all basic operations that a particular computer is capable of performing.

**Integer.** A whole number, which may be positive, negative, or zero.

**Iteration.** The processes of computation by repeated execution of a group of statements.

**Keyword.** A variable that has a value which relates to a mode of execution or the condition of the program, or depends on a particular machine.

**Label.** An identification of a statement for the purpose of transferring control during execution. See **goto.**

**Lexical order.** Alphabetical order.

**Line printer.** A mechanism that prints computer output one line at a time.

**Literal.** A data value that is presented explicitly in the program.

**Local variable.** A name whose value is saved when a defined function is called and restored when the function returns.

**Loop.** A section of program that transfers control back to its first statement.

**Memory.** Storage space. Any value that is directly referencable by the program through variables is in memory.

**Mixed mode.** An operation in which the operands have different data types, e.g., integer and real.

**Name.** A type of variable which consists simply of an identifier.

**Null string.** A string that contains no characters and whose length is zero.

**Number.** An integer or real number.

**Numeral string.** A string that represents a number.

**Object creation function.** A function that creates a defined data object.

**Operand.** An argument of an operation.

**Operating system.** An executive program that schedules and monitors the running of other programs on a computer.

**Operation.** A process that performs a computation.

**Operator.** A symbol which designates an operation. See **binary operator** and **unary operator**.

**Output.** The process of putting out data from a program.

**Output association.** A relationship between a variable and a data file which causes a record to be written on the file whenever a value is assigned to the variable.

**Page ejection.** An action of a line printer that causes a line of output to be printed at the top of the next page.

**Pattern.** A data object that specifies strings and relationships among strings.

**Pattern construction.** The process of creating a pattern.

**Pattern matching.** The process of comparing a pattern to a string to determine if the string has the structure specified by the pattern.

**Positional pattern.** A pattern that is concerned only with cursor position, not with the actual characters in a string.

**Precedence.** The property of a binary operator that determines how tightly it binds to its operands, in relation to other binary operators.

**Predicate.** A function that tests a relationship and fails if the specified relationship does not exist.

**Prefix notation.** A method of writing operations in which operators appear in front of their operands.

**Procedure.** A section of program executed when a defined function is called.

**Program.** An algorithm written in a language that can be run on a computer.

**Programmer-defined function.** See **defined function**.

**Programmer-defined data type.** See **defined data type**.

**Programming language.** A language that specifies operations to be executed on a computer.

**Real number.** In SNOBOL4, a decimal number.

**Record.** A unit of data in a file.

**Record length.** The number of characters in a record.

**Recursion.** A call of a defined function which results from execution of the function itself.

**Recursive function.** A function that uses recursion.

**Reference.** The way in which an element in an array or a table is accessed.

**Replacement.** Modification of a subject string, following successful pattern matching, in which the matched substring is replaced by another string.

**Sequential execution.** Execution of statements one after another, in the order in which they appear in a program.

**Statement.** A unit of a program which may perform assignment, pattern matching, or replacement.

**String.** A sequence of characters.

**String dump.** A listing of all names and their values, given on program termination.

**Subject.** The focus of attention in a statement, for the purpose of assignment, pattern matching, or replacement.

**Subscript.** A value used to reference an array or table.

**Subsequent.** A component of a pattern which follows another component. See **concatenation.**

**Substring.** A string which is part of another string.

**Success.** Satisfactory completion of an operation. See **failure.**

**Syntax.** The rules which determine the correct form for writing statements.

**Table.** A collection of variables referenced by value. See **array.**

**Termination.** The end of a program run.

**Trace association.** The designation of a name which is to be traced.

**Tracing.** A mode in which diagnostic information is automatically printed during execution.

**Trailing blanks.** Blanks on the right end of a string.

**Transfer of control.** Altering the ordinary sequential execution of statements to begin execution at another place in the program.

**Translator.** Loosely speaking, a system that converts a program in a programming language into a form that can be executed on a computer.

**Truncation.** Discarding of the remainder that results from division of two integers.

**Unanchored mode.** The mode of pattern matching in which a substring that is matched need not begin with the first character of the subject string. See **anchored mode.**

**Unary operator.** An operator that has one operand.

**Unconditional goto.** A goto that specifies transfer of control regardless of successful completion or failure in the statement in which it occurs. See **conditional goto**.

**Unevaluated expression.** An expression that is not executed until its value is required during pattern matching.

**Variable.** An object that has a value. Variables include names, array references, table references, keywords, and field functions.

# References


1. Griswold, R. E., J. P. Poage, and I. P. Polonsky, *The SNOBOL4 Programming Language*, 2nd ed. Prentice-Hall, Inc., Englewood Cliffs, N. J., 1971.

2. Sammet, Jean E., *Programming Languages: History and Fundamentals.* Prentice-Hall, Inc., Englewood Cliffs, N. J., 1969.

3. Griswold, R. E., *String and List Processing in SNOBOL4: Techniques and Applications.* Prentice-Hall, Inc. In preparation.

4. Griswold, R. E., *The Macro Implementation of SNOBOL4: A Case Study of Machine-Independent Software Development.* W. H. Freeman and Company, San Francisco, 1972.

5. Dewar, Robert B. K., "SPITBOL Version 2.0," *SNOBOL4 Project Document S4D23.* Illinois Institute of Technology, Chicago, February 12, 1971.

6. Newman, James R., *The World of Mathematics.* Simon and Schuster, New York, 1956. Vol. 1, pp. 718–719.

7. Vorobyov, N. N., *The Fibonacci Numbers.* Translated and adapted from the first Russian edition, 1951, by Norman D. Whaland, Jr. and Olga A. Titelbaum. D. C. Heath & Company, Boston, 1963.

8. Cowgill, George L., "Computer Applications in Archaeology," *Computers and the Humanities*, Vol. 2, No. 1 (September, 1967), pp. 17–23.

9. Chenhall, Robert G., "The Archaeological Data Bank: A Progress Report," *Computers and the Humanities*, Vol. 5, No. 3 (January, 1971), pp. 159–169.

10. Erickson, Raymond F., "Music Analysis and the Computer: A Report on Some Current Approaches and the Outlook for the Future," *Computers and the Humanities*, Vol. 3, No. 2 (November, 1968), pp. 87–104.

11. Lincoln, Harry B., "The Current State of Music Research and the Computer," *Computers and the Humanities*, Vol. 5, No. 1 (September, 1970), pp. 29–36.

12. Knuth, Donald E., *The Art of Computer Programming*, Volume 1: *Fundamental Algorithms.* Addison-Wesley, Reading, Mass., 1968.

# Index